P Young

THE
AMERICAN
REVOLUTIONARIES

A HISTORY
IN THEIR OWN WORDS
1750–1800

Also by Milton Meltzer

Soldiers in Washington's army as sketched in 1781 by Baron Ludwig von Closen. He was a Rhinelander attached as aide-de-camp to French General Rochambeau during the Yorktown campaign.

THE
AMERICAN
REVOLUTIONARIES

A HISTORY
IN THEIR OWN WORDS
1750–1800

EDITED BY

MILTON MELTZER

HarperTrophy®
A Division of HarperCollins*Publishers*

Picture Sources
Sources given are for the illustrations on the pages indicated. All other illustrations
are from the author's collection:
Library of Congress, 11; Frick Collection, 21; New York Public Library, Prints
Division, 55, 57; National Gallery of Art, 83; New-York Historical Society, 86;
Boston Athenaeum, 90; Historical Society of Pennsylvania, 95; Yale University Art
Gallery, 133; Museum of Fine Arts, Boston, 166; American Antiquarian Society,
171; Free Library of Pennsylvania, 195; New York Public Library Picture
Collection, 17, 25, 39, 40, 45, 47, 61, 63, 70, 71, 75, 99, 105, 107, 113, 117,
127, 135, 144, 160, 162, 175, 176, 183, 188, 190.

Library of Congress Cataloging-in-Publication Data
The American revolutionaries: a history in their own words (1750–1800)

Summary: Letter, diaries, memoirs, interviews, ballads, newspaper articles, and
speeches depict life and events in the American colonies in the second half of the
eighteenth century, with an emphasis on the years of the Revolutionary War.
   1. United States—History—Revolution, 1775–1783—Juvenile literature. 2.
United States—History—French and Indian War, 1755–1763—Juvenile literature.
3. United States—History—Confederation, 1783–1789—Juvenile literature. [1.
United States—History—Revolution, 1775–1783. 2. United States—Social life
and customs—Revolution, 1775–1783.] I. Meltzer, Milton, date
E208.A445   1987   973.3   86-47846
ISBN 0-690-04641-3
ISBN 0-690-04643-X (lib. bdg.)
ISBN 0-06-446145-9 (pbk.)

First Harper Trophy edition, 1993.

Harper Trophy® is a registered trademark
of HarperCollins Publishers Inc.

For Bill and Jane Langton

CONTENTS

FOREWORD

If you had lived at the time of the American Revolution, what would it have been like?

This book attempts to help you understand the Revolution as a human experience. It was people who made the Revolution, not abstract social and economic and political forces. Who were the new Americans? What did they hope for? What did they worry about? What was it like to meet the enemy in combat? What did the folks back home do as the men went off to fight? What did it feel like to make the modern world's first democratic republic and write its new Constitution?

The answers to these questions and many more are found in the personal documents left by those early Americans. In letters, diaries, journals, memoirs, interviews, ballads, newspapers, pamphlets, and speeches we find the first-person evidence of life in that last half of the eighteenth century: 1750–1800. The focus here is not so much on official papers as on the experiences of ordinary Americans, men or women, young and old. They speak in their own words.

I stress the youth of many of them. In George Washington's ranks there were messengers and cooks and drummers and waiters and, yes, fighters, who were only ten to fifteen years of age. Their stories, too, are in this book.

Introducing each voice is a note to identify the speaker and set the stage for his or her appearance. The people of that time spelled, capitalized, paragraphed, and punctuated somewhat differently from us. I have taken the liberty of modernizing their texts for the sake of easier reading. Cuts in the documents are indicated by ellipses (. . .). At the end of each document the source is given. The index will guide the reader to particular people, events, and topics.

THE
AMERICAN
REVOLUTIONARIES

A HISTORY
IN THEIR OWN WORDS
1750–1800

INTRODUCTION

FIRST, THE LAND: "So vast is the territory of North America," said Benjamin Franklin, "that it will require many ages to settle it fully." In the first one hundred and fifty years, the ragged line of settlements had run from Maine down to Georgia. Now, in 1750, it had yet to cross the Appalachians and plant communities in the unknown interior. In that wilderness only explorers, trappers, traders, and a handful of daring farmers risked treading on Indian territory. East of the mountains there were still vast tracts of unsettled lands. The forests were thick, the fields fertile, the shores and rivers alive with fish.

So the land was there, seeming unlimited in its reach. But idle land, raw land, turns a profit only when settlers come in to work it. The kings of Britain and their favorites had carved British North America into immense tracts of real estate. Privileged proprietors had thousands, hundreds of thousands, even millions of acres to

1

exploit for their own enrichment. They needed hands to cut down the trees, dig the soil, plant the seeds, harvest the crops.

It took a long time to people the land. In 1650 there were only 50,000 settlers—about as many as live in Pittsfield, Massachusetts, today—huddled mostly in Massachusetts and Virginia. A hundred years later the number had grown to 1,170,000. That is about the size of today's Detroit, Michigan. But for those times the leap in number was enormous. The colonial population was doubling about every twenty years. The largest concentration in 1750 was in the two tobacco colonies, Virginia and Maryland. The four New England colonies were next, followed by the middle colonies, and then the deep south.

Who came to America? Not the rich, not the nobility, nor the content. They stayed in Europe. Only some of the middle classes and more of the poor came. The well-to-do didn't want to risk what they had; the very poor were too demoralized to move. The people who emigrated were lured by cheap land and the dream of prosperity, or driven out by persecution, or forced against their will.

The immigrants were of many stocks. There were the English, the Scots, Welsh, Irish, the Dutch, French, Germans, the Swedes and Finns, the Swiss and Jews. A rich ethnic variety, but early on the English far outnumbered the other white colonials. And they were able to impose their language, their culture, their institutions of government and politics on the colonies. And this continued even when they lost their numerical dominance.

There never were enough willing immigrants to meet the needs of the new land. So other means of solving the problem were devised. One: Africans were brought here in chains, in ever-increasing numbers. Two: Persons without power were lured, forced, even kidnapped to the colonies. And three: If without money, they were brought over as indentured servants to work their way to freedom. The people of the British colonies were thus, by 1750, a blend of white and Black and Indian, of the free, the semifree, and the enslaved.

— 1 —

They Cry Out for Home

One who came in 1750 was Gottfried Mittelberger. He was a musician in Germany, asked to bring over an organ to a German congregation in a small town of Pennsylvania. From his home he traveled to Rotterdam, sailed to a stopover in England, and then on to Phila-delphia. Some four hundred passengers were packed into the same ship, most of them German and Swiss re-demptioners—that is, people pledged to work off the cost of passage. From his home to arrival in Philadelphia the trip took twenty-two weeks. He stayed four years in America, working as organist and schoolteacher. On his return to Germany he published an account of his experience. He was enraged by the lies and deceit he saw practised by the "newlanders"—the recruiting agents the shippers hired to tempt Europeans with false prom-ises. "Con men" we call them today; "soul sellers" they were called then. Mittelberger indicts the trade in white contract labor, and the sufferings inflicted upon them during their life in the colonies:

5

DURING THE JOURNEY the ship is full of pitiful signs of distress—smells, fumes, horrors, vomiting, various kinds of sea sickness, fever, dysentery, headaches, heat, constipation, boils, scurvy, cancer, mouth-rot, and similar afflictions, all of them caused by the age and the highly salted state of the food, especially of the meat, as well as by the very bad and filthy water, which brings about the miserable destruction and death of many. Add to all that shortage of food, hunger, thirst, frost, heat, dampness, fear, misery, vexation, and lamentation, as well as other troubles. Thus, for example, there are so many lice, especially on the sick people, that they have to be scraped off the bodies. All this misery reaches its climax when in addition to everything else one must also suffer through two to three days and nights of storm, with everyone convinced that the ship with all aboard is bound to sink. In such misery all the people on board pray and cry pitifully together. . . .

Among those who are in good health, impatience sometimes grows so great and bitter that one person begins to curse the other, or himself and the day of his birth, and people sometimes come close to murdering one another. Misery and malice are readily associated, so that people begin to cheat and steal from one another. And then one always blames the other for having undertaken the voyage. Often the children cry out against their parents, husbands against wives and wives against husbands, brothers against their sisters, friends and acquaintances against one another.

But most of all they cry out against the thieves of

human beings! Many groan and exclaim: "Oh! If only I were back at home, even lying in my pigsty!" Or they call out: "Ah, dear God, if I only once again had a piece of good bread or a good fresh drop of water." Many people whimper, sigh, and cry out pitifully for home. Most of them become homesick at the thought that many hundreds of people must necessarily perish, die, and be thrown into the ocean in such misery. And this in turn makes their families, or those who were responsible for their undertaking the journey, oftentimes fall almost into despair—so that it soon becomes practically impossible to rouse them from their depression. In a word, groaning, crying, and lamentation go on aboard day and night—so that even the hearts of the most hardened, hearing all this, begin to bleed.

One can scarcely conceive what happens at sea to women in childbirth and to their innocent offspring. Very few escape with their lives; and mother and child, as soon as they have died, are thrown into the water. On board our ship, on a day on which we had a great storm, a woman about to give birth, and unable to deliver under the circumstances, was pushed through one of the portholes into the sea because her corpse was far back in the stern and could not be brought forward to the deck.

Children between the ages of one and seven seldom survive the sea voyage; and parents must often watch their offspring suffer miserably, die, and be thrown into the ocean from want, hunger, thirst, and the like. I myself, alas, saw such a pitiful fate overtake thirty-two children on board our vessel, all of whom were finally thrown into the sea. Their parents grieve all the more, since their children do not find repose in the earth, but are devoured by the predatory fish of the ocean. It is also worth noting that children who have not had either measles or smallpox usually get them on board the ship and for the most part perish as a result.

On one of these voyages a father often becomes infected by his wife and children, or a mother by her small children, or even both parents by their children, or sometimes whole families one by the other, so that many times numerous corpses lie on the cots next to those who are still alive, especially when contagious diseases rage on board.

Many other accidents also occur on these ships, especially falls in which people become totally crippled and can never be completely made whole again. Many also tumble into the sea.

It is not surprising that many passengers fall ill, because in addition to all the other troubles and miseries, warm food is served only three times a week, and at that is very bad, very small in quantity, and so dirty as to be hardly palatable at all. And the water distributed in these ships is often very black, thick with dirt, and full of worms. Even when very thirsty, one is almost unable to drink it without loathing. It is certainly true that at sea one would often spend a great deal of money just for one good piece of bread, or one good drink of water— not even to speak of a good glass of wine—if one could only obtain them. I have, alas, had to experience that myself. For toward the end of the voyage we had to eat the ship's biscuit, which had already been spoiled for a long time, even though in no single piece was there more than the size of a thaler that was not full of red worms and spiders' nests. True, great hunger and thirst teach one to eat and drink everything—but many must forfeit their lives in the process. It is impossible to drink sea water, since it is salty and bitter as gall. If this were not the case, one could undertake such an ocean voyage with far less expense and without so many hardships.

When at last after the long and difficult voyage the ships finally approach land, when one gets to see the headlands for the sight of which the people on board had longed so passionately, then everyone crawls from below to the deck, in order to look at the land from afar. And people cry for joy, pray, and sing praises and thanks to God. The glimpse of land revives the passengers, especially those who are half dead of illness. Their spirits, however weak they had become, leap up, triumph, and rejoice within them. Such people are now willing to bear all ills patiently, if only they can disembark soon and step on land. But, alas, alas!

When the ships finally arrive in Philadelphia after the long voyage, only those are let off who can pay their sea freight or can give good security. The others, who lack the money to pay, have to remain on board until they are purchased and until their purchasers can thus pry them loose from the ship. In this whole process the sick are the worst off, for the healthy are preferred and are more readily paid for. The miserable people who are ill must often still remain at sea and in sight of the city for another two or three weeks—which in many cases means death. Yet many of them, were they able to pay their debts and to leave the ships at once, might escape with their lives. . . .

This is how the commerce in human beings on board ship takes place. Every day, Englishmen, Dutchmen, and High Germans come from Philadelphia and other places, some of them very far away, sometimes twenty or thirty or forty hours' journey, and go on board the newly arrived vessel that has brought people from Europe and offers them for sale. From among the healthy they pick out those suitable for the purposes for which they require them. Then they negotiate with them as to the length of the period for which they will go into service in order to pay off their passage, the whole amount of which they generally still owe. When an agreement has been reached, adult persons by written contract bind themselves to serve for three, four, five, or six years, according to their health and age. The very young, between the ages of ten and fifteen, have to serve until they are twenty-one, however.

Many parents, in order to pay their fares in this way and get off the ship, must barter and sell their children as if they were cattle. Since the fathers and mothers often do not know where or to what masters their children are to be sent, it frequently happens that after leaving the vessel, parents and children do not see each other for years on end, or even for the rest of their lives.

People who arrive without the funds to pay their way

Early immigrants from Scandinavia settled in Delaware and built the first log cabins.

and who have children under the age of five cannot settle their debts by selling them. They must give away these children for nothing to be brought up by strangers; and in return these children must stay in service until they are twenty-one years old. Children between five and ten who owe half fare, that is, thirty florins, must also go into service in return until they are twenty-one years old, and can neither set free their parents nor take their debts upon themselves. On the other hand, the sale of children older than ten can help to settle a part of their parents' passage charges.

A wife must be responsible for her sick husband and

a husband for his sick wife, and pay his or her fare respectively, and must thus serve five to six years not only for herself or himself, but also for the spouse, as the case may be. If both should be ill on arrival, then such persons are brought directly from the ship into a hospital, but not until it is clear that no purchaser for them is to be found. As soon as they have recovered, they must serve to pay off their fare, unless they have the means immediately to discharge the debt.

It often happens that whole families—husband, wife, and children—being sold to different purchasers, become separated, especially when they cannot pay any part of the passage money. When either the husband or the wife has died at sea, having come more than halfway, then the surviving spouse must pay not only his or her fare, but must also pay for or serve out the fare of the deceased.

When both parents have died at sea, having come more than halfway, then their children, especially when they are still young and have nothing to pawn or cannot pay, must be responsible for their own fares as well as those of their parents, and must serve until they are twenty-one years old. Once free of service, they receive a suit of clothing as a parting gift, and if it has been so stipulated the men get a horse and the women a cow. . . .

Occupations vary, but work is strenuous in this new land; and many who have just come into the country at an advanced age must labor hard for their bread until they die. I will not even speak of the young people. Most jobs involve cutting timber, felling oak trees, and leveling, or as one says there, clearing, great tracts of forest, roots and all. Such forest land, having been cleared in this way, is then laid out in fields and meadows. From the best wood that has been felled people construct railings or fences around the new fields. Inside these, all meadows, all lawns, gardens, and orchards, and all arable lands, are surrounded and enclosed by thickly cut wood planks set in zigzag fashion one above the other. And thus cattle, horses, and sheep are confined to pastureland.

Our Europeans who have been purchased must work hard all the time. For new fields are constantly being laid out; and thus they learn from experience that oak-tree stumps are just as hard in America as they are in Germany. In these hot regions there is particularly fulfilled in them that with which the Lord God afflicted man in the first book of Moses, on account of his sin and disobedience, namely: "Thou shalt eat thy bread in the sweat of thy brow." Thus let him who wants to earn his piece of bread honestly and in a Christian manner and who can only do this by manual labor in his native country stay there rather than come to America.

For, in the first place, things are no better in Pennsylvania. However hard one may have had to work in his native land, conditions are bound to be equally tough or even tougher in the new country. Furthermore the emigrant has to undertake the arduous voyage, which means not only that he must suffer more misery for half a year than he would have to suffer doing the hardest labor, but also that he must spend approximately two hundred florins which no one will refund to him. If he has that much money, he loses it; if he does not have it, he must work off his debt as a slave or as a miserable servant. So let people stay in their own country and earn their keep honestly for themselves and their families. Furthermore, I want to say that those people who may let themselves be talked into something and seduced into the voyage by the thieves of human beings are the biggest fools if they really believe that in America or Pennsylvania roasted pigeons are going to fly into their mouths without their having to work for them.

How sad and miserable is the fate of so many thousand German families who lost all the money they ever owned in the course of the long and difficult voyage, many of whom perished wretchedly and had to be buried at sea and who, once they had arrived in the new country, saw their old and young separated and sold away into places far removed one from the other! The saddest aspect of all this is that in most instances parents must give away their young children, getting nothing in return. For such children are destined never to see or recognize parents, brothers, and sisters again, and, after they have been sold to strangers, are not brought up in any sort of Christian faith. . . .

From *Journey to Pennsylvania*, Gottfried Mittelberger, 1756.

2

Whipped Like an Animal

From a female servant in Maryland comes this forlorn letter to her father, John Sprigs, in London. One could guess that young Elizabeth Sprigs had left home without permission, and gone to America as an indentured servant. Perhaps she did it to break free of her family and stand on her own two feet. But the promise of adventure and independence turned sour:

MARYLAND, SEPTEMBER 22ND, 1756.

Honored Father:

My being forever banished from your sight will, I hope, pardon the boldness I now take of troubling you with this. My long silence has been purely owing to my undutifullness to you, and well knowing I had offended in the highest degree, put a tie to my tongue and pen, for fear I should be extinct from your good graces and add a further trouble to you. But too well knowing your care and tenderness for me, so long as I retained my duty to you, induced me once again to endeavor, if possible, to kindle up that flame again. O dear father, believe what I am going to relate, the words of truth and sincerity, and balance my former bad conduct [to] my sufferings

15

here, and then I am sure you'll pity your distressed daughter. What we unfortunate English people suffer here is beyond the probability of you in England to conceive. Let it suffice that I, one of the unhappy number, am toiling almost day and night, and very often in horse's drudgery, with only this comfort, that "You bitch, you do not half enough!" and then tied up and whipped to that degree that you'd not serve an animal. Scarce anything but Indian corn and salt to eat, and that even begrudged. Nay, many Negroes are better used. Almost naked, no shoes nor stockings to wear, and the comfort after slaving during master's pleasure, what rest we can get is to wrap ourselves up in a blanket and lie upon the ground. This is the deplorable condition your poor Betty endures, and now I beg, if you have any bowels of compassion left, show it by sending me some relief. Clothing is the principal thing wanting, which if you should condescend to, may easily send them to me by any of the ships bound to Baltimore Town, Patapsco River, Maryland. Give me leave to conclude in duty to you and uncles and aunts, and respect to all friends.

Honored Father,
your undutifull and disobedient child,
Elizabeth Sprigs

From *Colonial Captivities, Marches, and Journeys.* Isabel Calder, ed. Macmillan, 1935.

Because of the harsh conditions many indentured servants ran away. It was their most common crime, and

This Indenture Made

Day of *may* in the Year of our Lord God, One Thousand Seven Hundred, and *seventy one* BETWEEN *Nathan Symmons Marriner* of the one Part, and *Michael Croak*

of the other Part, WITNESSETH, that the said *Michael Croak* do hereby Covenant, Promise and Grant, to and with the *Nathan Symmons* his Executors, Administrators and Assigns, from the Day of the Date hereof, until the first and next arrival in America, and after, for and during the Term of *four* Years, to serve in such Service and Employment as the said *Nathan Symmons* or his Assigns, shall there employ *him* according to the Custom of the Country, of the like kind. In consideration whereof, the said *Nathan Symmons* doth hereby Covenant and Grant to and with the said *Michael Croak* to pay for *his* Passage, and to find and allow Meat, Drink, Apparel and Lodging, with other Necessaries, during the said Term ; and at the End of the said Term to pay unto *him* the usual Allowance, according to the Custom of the Country in the like Kind.

In Witness whereof, the parties above-mentioned to these Indentures, have interchangeably set their Hands and Seals, in the City of Waterford, where Stampt-Paper is not used, the Day and Year above written.

Signed, Sealed and Delivered, in the Presence of

Michael Croak

An indenture agreement made in 1771. The immigrant pledges himself to four years of labor in America in exchange for his ship passage and his food, clothing, and lodging during his term of service.

one not easy to get away with. Everyone in the colonies had to carry a pass—an identity card. If you were not where you were supposed to be, the penalties were stiff: fines, whippings, extra service of two to ten times what the master had lost in your absence. A captured servant who was not claimed would be sold at public auction. All bonded servants were the property of their masters. The difference between that and slavery? Bonded servants by contract had a limit to their service and had some legal rights. Slaves were bound for life, and so were their descendants, forever.

Did indentured servants do better when their contracts came to an end? Not very many. Only one out of ten, according to the estimates, became a substantial farmer and another one an artisan. That leaves eight who died in servitude, went back to England, or elsewhere, when their term of labor was finished, or faded away to become the "poor whites" of town or countryside. Freed servants were in poor physical or mental shape to start life over again. Not until well after the Revolution did the various forms of unfree labor decline.

Here are some advertisements for runaway servants placed in local papers by anxious masters. Note that all these happen to be convicts. Offenders in England at this time were punished by being shipped to the colonies for a term of labor. Perhaps 30,000 felons arrived in America in the 1700s, most of them taken on by the poorer planters in the south:

RUN AWAY from tne Subscriber, of Essex County, on Wednesday the 9th of this . . . November, a convict ser-

18

vant woman, named Ann Wheatley; who is a lusty, well-set woman, with very dark hair, black eyes, and a fresh complexion. . . .

From the *Virginia Gazette*, Friday, November 11–Friday, November 18, 1737.

RUN AWAY from the subscriber, living in Fairfax County, on the 30th day of March last, an English convict servant woman, named Isabella Pierce; of a middle stature, thin visage, limps with her right leg, which, if examined, will appear to be a large scar on each side of the ankle of her said leg. . . .

From the *Virginia Gazette*, Friday, May 2–Friday, May 9, 1745.

RUN AWAY from the subscriber, in Northumberland County, two Irish convict servants named William and Hannah Daylies, tinkers by trade, of which the woman is extremely good; they had a note of leave to go out and work in Richmond County and Hobb's Hole, the money to be paid to Job Thomas, in said county; soon after I heard they were run away. . . .

From the *Virginia Gazette*, March 26, 1767.

3

The Men Were So Panic Struck

Like a quarrel between members of a family, the conflict that developed between Great Britain and America became very bitter. Britain was like a parent insisting on ruling its child in the old ways and America the child defiantly insisting it was big enough to decide its own course. As the mother country, Britain looked upon the American colonies as possessions totally under her control.

When first settled, the colonies were glad to have British protection—especially because Spain and France were building empires next door, on the same continent. Britain gave advice and orders on what the colonies should grow and export, and ruled early on that British ships should carry colonial goods to the home country, thus cutting out foreign competition. Such close supervision soon became a nuisance, and colonial merchants dodged it by smuggling goods abroad on their own ships. It meant that Americans made fatter profits at British expense.

So money was one source of trouble between Britain and her colonies. Another was government. Three levels of it were operating in the colonies at that time: One was the way King and Parliament controlled the colonies and protected them. Another was how the government of each colony dealt with the internal issues: taxation, improving roads and ferries, granting land, building defense. And the third was the way the government in each town or village enforced laws, conducted elections, cared for the poor, and resolved local problems or issues.

When the European powers fought for world domination, the conflict spilled over into America. In 1755 North America became the central theater of a struggle between France and Britain. It was called the French and Indian War here. (In Europe, the Seven Years' War.) It was a long struggle that ended when the British defeated the French and drove them from North America.

That victory was a joint effort: the British and Americans fought side by side, but with the British in charge. Both wanted to keep France from expanding into the rich lands beyond the Appalachians. The colonials wished to eliminate business rivals, take over the fur trade from the French, gain fresh farmlands, and secure their frontier from the Indians armed by the French.

The colonists and the British had more people and resources in America than the French. But they were not unified and fought poorly, and the French won the first battles. A bad defeat came on July 9, 1755, when the French and their Indian allies ambushed General Braddock's British and colonial troops seven miles from Fort Duquesne (now Pittsburgh). The shocking setback was reported in a journal kept by a British officer. His name, rank, and regiment are unknown, but his details are vivid:

WEDNESDAY JULY the 9th. As we were to cross the Monongahela that day and so near the fort as we were drawing, it was found absolutely necessary to detach a party to secure the crossing. Accordingly Lieutenant Colonel Gage with 300 men and the grenadier company with two pieces of cannon marched before daybreak and before the road was cleared. At daybreak the whole detachment marched, though slowly, having a great deal of trouble with the road. After 5 miles' march we came to the first crossing of the river, which was extremely fine, having a view of at least 4 miles up the river and the breadth about 600 yards. Near this first crossing our advanced party scared some Indians from their holes, finding many spears and their fires newly burning.

From this crossing to the other was near two miles and much the finest of the two; on the other side of the second crossing the advanced party had halted at Frazier's house close to the bank, which was very steep and took us two hours to make it passable for the carriages. The General now thinking the dangerous passes were over, did not suffer the advanced party to proceed any farther than the distance of a few yards from the main body. It was proposed to strengthen the flanks but this was unhappily rejected.

Between 12 and 1 after we had marched 800 yards from the river, our first flank upon the left was fired on and every man of them killed or wounded. The alarm quickly became general and the fire was brisk from right to left. The Indians were all planted behind trees and fired with the utmost security; the ground where the enemy was posted was rising and advantageous. Upon our right were a couple of immense large trees fallen on each other which the Indians were in possession of and annoyed us very much. But an officer and a party of men soon dislodged them, and by a pretty brisk fire kept our right tolerably easy; the guns, which were all rather to the left, fired both round and grapeshot, doing great execution.

The Indians, whether ordered or not I cannot say, kept an incessant fire on the guns and killed the men very fast. These Indians from their irregular method of fighting by running from one place to another obliged us to wheel from right to left, to desert the guns and then hastily to return and cover them.

At the first of the firing the General, who was at the head of the detachment, came to the front, and the American troops, though without any orders, ran up immediately, some behind trees and others into the ranks, and put the whole in confusion. The men, from what stories they had heard of the Indians in regard to their scalping and tomahawking, were so panic struck that their officers had little or no command over them, and if any got a shot at one, the fire immediately ran through the whole line, though they saw nothing but trees. The whole body was frequently divided into several parties, and then they were sure to fire on one another.

The greatest part of the men who were behind trees were either killed or wounded by our own people; even one or two officers were killed by their own platoons. Such was the confusion that the men were sometimes

20 or 30 deep, and he thought himself securest who was in the center. During all this time the enemy kept a continual fire and every shot took place. The General had given orders that they should fire in platoons (which was impossible to be effected), which would not have answered at all as the enemy were situated.

Within about two hours and a half the men were obliged (or at least did) retreat three or four times and were as often rallied. We found that we should never gain the day unless we dislodged them from the rising ground, upon which Lieutenant Colonel Burton with the grenadiers pushed and attempted the hill. For some time we were in hopes of their success, but some shot killing 2 or 3 of them, the rest retreated very fast, leaving their officers entreating and commanding but without any regard to what they said.

The Indians were scalping at the beginning of the affair, which we heard was a sign they were dubious of success, but it is certain they never gave ground. General Braddock, who was in the heat of the action the whole time, was greatly exposed: he had 4 horses shot under him and was shot through several parts of his clothes. At the latter end of the affair an unlucky shot hit him in the body, which occasioned his death in 3 or 4 days afterward.

After the men retreated from the hill, they made some stand and the cannon kept a tolerable good fire. But very soon, for want of a sufficient guard to it, the men were obliged to leave them [the cannon]. During this time the wagoners, who imagined things would turn out badly,

The British General Braddock, wounded in ambush by the French and their Indian allies, is carried off the field of slaughter.

had taken the gear from their horses and galloped quite away, so that if fortune had turned in our favor we had not one horse left to draw the train forward.

However, after about 4 hours of incessant firing and two-thirds of the men killed or wounded, they, as if by beat of drum, turned to the right about and made a most precipitate retreat, every one trying who should be the first. The enemy pursued us, butchering as they came, as far as the other side of the river. During our crossing, they shot many in the water, both men and women, and dyed the stream with their blood, scalping and cutting them in a most barbarous manner. On the other side of the river we most of us halted to resolve on what to do.

But the men, being so terrified, desired to go on, nay, indeed they would. Melancholy situation!—expecting every moment to have our retreat cut off (which half a dozen men would easily have done), and a certainty of meeting no provisions for 60 miles.

I must observe that our retreat was so hasty that we were obliged to leave the whole train—ammunition, provision, and baggage—to the plundering of the Indians. The men's wounds being fresh, many of them retreated with us though in the utmost agonies. In making the road we had marked the trees on each side of it, which we found of very great use to us in our retreat, for being obliged to keep marching the whole night through a continued wood, the people frequently lost their way, and had nothing to put them right except feeling for the marks. Nevertheless many of the rear lost their way, and of the wounded entirely lost. The General in the night found himself extremely bad, so they contrived a kind of litter to be carried on men's shoulders. It was with the utmost difficulty they could get men to carry him on, though large promises were made. The men indeed had not eaten anything since very early on the day of the action nor had one moment's rest, which was some (though small) excuse.

From *The Journal of a British Officer*, Charles Hamilton, ed.

That defeat was a turning point for young George Washington, an aide to General Braddock. He lost faith in England's wisdom and military skill. In a letter to his mother nine days after the disaster he gave this brief account of what had happened:

FORT CUMBERLAND, JULY 18, 1755

Honour'd Mad'm:

As I doubt not but you have heard of our defeat, and perhaps have it represented in a worse light (if possible) than it deserves; I have taken this earliest opportunity to give you some account of the engagement, as it happened within 7 miles of the French fort, on Wednesday the 9th.

We marched on to that place without any considerable loss, having only now and then a straggler picked up by the French scouting Indian. When we came there, we were attacked by a body of French and Indians, whose number (I am certain) did not exceed 300 men; ours consisted of about 1,300 well-armed troops, chiefly of the English soldiers, who were struck with such a panic that they behaved with more cowardice than it is possible to conceive. The officers behaved gallantly in order to encourage their men, for which they suffered greatly—there being near 60 killed and wounded—a large proportion out of the number we had! The Virginia troops showed a good deal of bravery, and were near all killed; for, I believe, out of 3 companies that were there, there is scarce 30 men left alive; Captain Peyrouny and all his officers down to a corporal was killed; Captain Polson shared near as hard a fate, for only one of his was left. In short, the dastardly behavior of those

27

they call regulars exposed all others that were inclined to do their duty to almost certain death; and at last, in despite of all the efforts of the officers to the contrary, they broke and run as sheep pursued by dogs, and it was impossible to rally them.

The General was wounded, of which he died 3 days after. Sir Peter Halket was killed in the field where died many other brave officers; I luckily escaped without a wound, though I had four bullets through my coat, and two horses shot under me. Captains Orme and Morris, two of the General's Aides de Camp, were wounded early in the engagement, which rendered the duty hard upon me, as I was the only person then left to distribute the General's orders, which I was scarcely able to do, as I was not half recovered from a violent illness that confined me to my bed, and a wagon, for above 10 days. I am still in a weak and feeble condition, which induces me to halt here, 2 or 3 days, in hopes of recovering a little strength to enable me to proceed homewards— from whence, I fear I shall not be able to stir till towards September, so that I shall not have the pleasure of seeing you till then, unless it be in Fairfax. Please to give my love to Mr. Lewis and my sister, and compliments to Mr. Jackson and all other friends that inquire after me. I am, Hon'd Madam, your most dutiful son.

From *Affectionately Yours, George Washington*,
Thomas Fleming, ed., 1968.

4

I Believe Liberty
Is the Slave's Right

In the mid-1700s the largest stream of immigration was that of black slaves. By 1770 the black population in the colonies had grown to nearly half a million. Most of the slaves were bought by whites from native African slavers on or near the West African coast. Slavery in Africa had existed long before whites came there. But once the European slave trade began, the profits to be made from selling slaves abroad led native kings to make a legal business of it. Several European nations engaged in the trade, but England took control of the trade to her American colonies in the early 1700s, making great profits from it. The transatlantic passage was terrible, costing untold thousands of lives from revolts, suicides, and above all, disease on shipboard.

Slavery in the colonies was concentrated mainly in the south, with Blacks working on the plantations, in domestic service, or in the crafts. Tobacco, cotton, sugar, rice, and indigo were the chief crops worked by gangs of slave labor the year round. Only a small number of the richest planters owned a hundred or more slaves. The vast majority of slaveholders had twenty or fewer.

North of Maryland slavery was not crucial to the economy. Slaves were most numerous in New York, with

29

fewer in New England and the other northern colonies. But New England shipowners were the major carriers of the slave trade to the mainland colonies. They became wealthy and powerful. So respectable was the business of buying and selling humans that even the most eminent religious leaders, such as Jonathan Edwards and the Mathers, owned slaves. Slaves in the north did all kinds of work, skilled and unskilled. They worked in households and on farms, and for printers, carpenters, tanners, distillers, blacksmiths, shipbuilders. Many went to sea.

In the 1700s slavery became firmly fixed in the colonial economy. It shaped rapidly into the form it held until the Civil War. It was wrapped in a system of beliefs and practises, rooted in racism. Blackness to the white English had had a negative image for centuries. It meant dirt, disease, disaster, death. People took a black skin to be a sign of punishment for terrible sin. And were not the African Blacks heathens, not Christians? The explorers and traders who came to the coast of Africa saw the native peoples simply as naked savages with no culture or civilization worth attention.

Of course such ignorance and prejudice made it easy to develop excuses for enslaving the Africans. It would be a kindness to the Blacks to civilize and Christianize them. The fat profits to be made from the trade—that was only business. The English colonials never thought of treating Blacks, even free Blacks, as equals. They never considered setting a time limit to their servitude, or giving them any rights, as they did with white indentured servants. So slavery became the bedrock of the southern economy and society.

But not everyone accepted it. The Blacks never did. They spoke up for their freedom as early as 1661. Their resistance took many forms, from running away to revolt. And some whites, too, felt bondage was wrong and should be done away with. Samuel Sewall's 1700 pamphlet The Selling of Joseph *began with these words: "For as much as liberty is in real value next unto life: none ought to part with it themselves or deprive others of it. . . ."*

Men like Anthony Benezet, Dr. Benjamin Rush, and Benjamin Franklin openly encouraged Blacks to seek the abolition of slavery. It was the Quaker John Woolman who roused the Friends to the cause of black freedom. Born in 1720, in New Jersey, he was a tailor by trade. Asked by his employer to draw up a bill of sale for a Black, his conscience troubled him. But he did it, while telling seller and buyer he felt slavery to be wrong. From that time on he refused to have any part of actions that bolstered slavery. He traveled south, and what he saw of the terrible effects of slavery in Maryland and Virginia moved him to write against it. He urged Quakers and others to give up their slaves. He became convinced that human greed for property was at the root of slavery, of war, and of all social evils. He died of smallpox in 1772. These passages on slavery are taken from his journal, published two years after his death. It is considered to be the first American classic:

9TH OF 5TH MONTH [1757]. Breakfasted at a friend's house who, afterward, putting us a little on our way . . . I had conversation with him, in the fear of the Lord, concerning his slaves, in which my heart was tender, and I used much plainness of speech with him, which he appeared to take it kindly. . . .

On the way, happening in company with a Colonel of the militia, who appeared to be a thoughtful man, I took occasion to remark on the difference in general betwixt a people used to labor moderately for their living, training up their children in frugality and business, and those who live on the labor of slaves; the former, in my view, being the most happy life. He concurred in the remark, and mentioned the trouble arising from the untoward, slothful disposition of the Negroes, adding that one of our laborers would do as much in a day as two of their slaves. I replied that free men whose minds were properly on their business found a satisfaction in the improving, cultivating, and providing for their families; but Negroes, laboring to support those who claim them as their property, and expecting nothing but slavery during life, had not the like inducement to be industrious.

After some further conversation I said that men having power too often misapplied it; that though we made slaves of the Negroes, and the Turks made slaves of the Christians, I believed that liberty was the natural right of all men equally. This he did not deny, but said the lives of the Negroes were so wretched in their own country that many of them lived better here than there. I only said, "There's great odds in regard to us on what principle we act"; and so the conversation on that head ended.

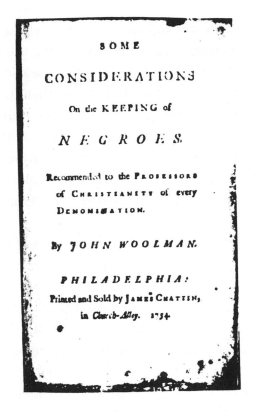

Title page of John Woolman's first antislavery essay.

I may here add that another person some time afterward mentioned the wretchedness of the Negroes occasioned by their intestine [sic] wars as an argument in favor of our fetching them away for slaves. To which I replied, if compassion for the Africans, on account of their domestic troubles, was the real motive of our purchasing them, that spirit of tenderness being attended to would incite us to use them kindly, that as strangers brought out of affliction their lives might be happy among us. And, as they are human creatures whose souls are as precious as ours, and who may receive the same help and comfort from the Holy Scriptures as we do, we could not omit suitable endeavors to instruct them therein; but while we manifest by our conduct that our views in purchasing them are to advance ourselves, and while our buying captives taken in war animates those parties to push on that war and increase desolation amongst them, to say they live unhappy in Africa is far from being an argument in our favor.

I further said, the present circumstances of these provinces to me appear difficult; the slaves look like a burdensome stone to such as burden themselves with them; and that if the white people retain a resolution to prefer their own outward prospect of gain to all other considerations, and do not act conscientiously toward them as fellow creatures, I believe that burden will grow heavier and heavier until times change in a way disagreeable to us. At which the person appeared very serious and acknowledged that, in considering their condition and the manner of their treatment in these provinces, he had sometimes thought it might be just in the Almighty to so order it.

Having traveled on a direct line through Maryland, we came amongst friends at Cedar Creek in Virginia on the 12th; and the next day rode in company with several of them a day's journey to Camp Creek. . . . Soon after a friend in company began to talk in support of the slave trade, and said the Negroes were understood to be the offspring of Cain, their blackness being the mark of God

Anthony Benezet, a Pennsylvania Quaker, joined John Woolman in opposing slavery. He taught black children out of antislavery textbooks he wrote himself.

set upon him after he murdered Abel his brother, that it was the design of Providence they should be slaves, as a condition proper to the race of so wicked a man as Cain was. Then another spoke in support of what had been said. To all which I replied as follows: that Noah and his family were all who survived the flood according to Scripture; and, as Noah was of Seth's race, the family of Cain was wholly destroyed. One of them said that after the flood Ham went to the land of Nod and took a wife; that Nod was a land far distant inhabited by Cain's race, and that the flood did not reach it; and as Ham was sentenced to be a servant of servants to his brethren, these two families, being thus joined, were undoubtedly fit only for slaves.

I replied, the flood was a judgment upon the world for their abominations, and it was granted that Cain's stock was the most wicked, and therefore unreasonable to suppose that they were spared. As to Ham's going to the land of Nod for a wife, no time being fixed, Nod might be inhabited by some of Noah's family before Ham married the second time; moreover, the text saith expressly, "That all flesh died that moved upon the earth." I further reminded them how the prophets repeatedly declare, "That the son shall not suffer for the iniquity of the father, but every one be answerable for his own sins." I was troubled to perceive the darkness of their imaginations, and in some pressure of spirit said, "The love of ease and gain are the motives in general of keeping slaves, and men are wont to take hold of weak arguments to support a cause which is unreasonable. I've no interest on either side save only the interest which I desire to have in the truth. I believe liberty is their right, and as I see they are not only deprived of it, but treated in other respects with inhumanity in many places, I believe He who is a refuge for the oppressed will, in His own time, plead their cause, and happy will it be for such as walk in uprightness before Him." Thus our conversation ended. . . .

From *Journal of John Woolman*, Janet Whitney, ed., 1950.

5

We Are Not Bound
to Yield Obedience

Despite the disaster near Duquesne, the French and In-
dian War ended in a British victory. It added vast ter-
ritory to the empire. The colonies shared in the triumph.
They had learned to cooperate with one another during
the long struggle, and felt their growing strength. Some
thought they need not depend any longer on Britain to
defend themselves. The new territory acquired in battle
promised to take care of the shortage of farmland.

But when Indian uprisings threatened the frontiers,
Britain barred the colonists from crossing the Alleghe-
nies into what is now the midwest. How and when to
settle the west was but one dispute that grew out of the
military victory. Who would administer the expanding
American empire? Who would pay the war debts? Why
should the colonists have to sell their raw materials only
to England and buy only English products?

And didn't the colonists have the right to make their
own decisions? The British Parliament since the English
Revolution of the seventeenth century had taken a greater
role in deciding domestic and foreign policy. The col-
onies were linked to England through the Crown. It was
the king who had given them their charters, defined their
borders, and authorized their governments. The colonial

governors still took their orders from the king or his officials.

The colonies had welcomed the rise of parliamentary power. But now they worried over how much that power should determine their lives on this side of the Atlantic. Could Parliament do whatever it wanted to shape colonial policy, even though the colonists had no voice in Parliament? Or was there a limit to Parliament's authority? Soon the extent of that power became the big issue. British leaders would accept no limits on Parliament's power. The colonies would gradually take the opposite view: Parliament had no authority over them.

Money issues became mixed with political issues. Britain was faced with a heavy postwar debt, rising taxes at home, and the burden of supporting an army in America. In 1764 Parliament passed the Sugar Act, the first law to raise money in the colonies for the Crown. The law taxed various products, restricted others, and strengthened the customs service to enforce the trade laws. It'll ruin our economy! the colonists cried. A Boston town meeting denounced "taxation without representation," and called on the colonies to unite in protest. Then in 1765 the colonies were ordered to provide barracks and supplies for the British troops. On top of that came the Stamp Act, placing a direct tax upon newspapers, almanacs, pamphlets, broadsides, legal documents, dice, and playing cards. Even a boy graduating from school had to pay for a stamp on his diploma. The money would go for defense of the colonies.

The measure only raised higher the fires of protest. In Virginia, newly elected Patrick Henry, tall, red-haired,

Patrick Henry, the fiery radical who spoke for the frontier people before the Virginia assembly. He served in the Continental Congress and then as Governor of Virginia.

*shabbily dressed, and only twenty-nine, introduced res-
olutions asserting that no one but the assembly had the
right to lay taxes upon the colony. "If this be treason,
make the most of it!" he cried out. When published, his
resolves ignited debate countrywide, and other colonies
soon followed Virginia's lead:*

WHEREAS, the Honorable House of Commons, in England, have of late drawn into question how far the General Assembly of this colony hath power to enact laws

39

for laying of taxes and imposing duties payable by the people of this, His Majesty's most ancient colony; for settling . . . the same to all future times, the House of Burgesses of this present General Assembly have come to the following resolves:

[1.] Resolved: That the first adventurers and settlers of this His Majesty's colony and dominion brought with them, and transmitted to their posterity . . . all the privileges, franchises, and immunities that have at any time been held, enjoyed, and possessed by the people of Great Britain.

[2.] Resolved: That by two royal charters, granted by King James the First, the colonists aforesaid are declared entitled to all the privileges, liberties, and immunities of denizens and natural-born subjects, to all intents and purposes as if they had been abiding and born within the realm of England.

[3.] Resolved: That the taxation of the people by themselves, or by persons chosen by themselves to represent them, who [can] only know what taxes the people are

The Stamp Act forced the colonists to buy and use stamps such as these to show they had paid the hated taxes.

able to bear, and the easiest mode of raising them, and are equally affected by such taxes themselves, is the distinguishing characteristic of British freedom, and without which the ancient Constitution cannot subsist.

[4.] Resolved: That his Majesty's liege people of this most ancient colony have uninterruptedly enjoyed the right of being thus governed by their own Assembly in the article of their taxes and internal police, and that the same hath never been forfeited . . . but hath been constantly recognized by the kings and people of Great Britain.

[5.] Resolved, therefore: That the General Assembly of this colony have the only and sole exclusive right and power to lay taxes . . . upon the inhabitants of this colony, and that every attempt to vest such power in any person or persons whatsoever, other than the General Assembly aforesaid, has a manifest tendency to destroy British [as] well as American freedom.

[6.] Resolved: That his Majesty's liege people, the inhabitants of this colony, are not bound to yield obedience to any law or ordinance whatever designed to impose any taxation whatsoever upon them, other than the laws or ordinances of the General Assembly aforesaid.

[7.] Resolved: That any person who shall by speaking or writing, assert or maintain that any person or persons, other than the General Assembly of this colony, have any right or power to impose or lay any taxation on the people here, shall be deemed an enemy to his Majesty's colony.

From *Journals of the House of Burgesses of Virginia, 1761–1765*, J. D. Kennedy, ed.

6

Seventeen Hundred Levellers with Firearms

To make sure the Stamp Act was not obeyed, groups of men organized in each colony, calling themselves the Sons of Liberty. Men appointed to collect the stamp tax were pressured, if necessary with threats of violence, to resign their posts. In Boston the Sons of Liberty forced their way into Lieutenant Governor Thomas Hutchinson's mansion, wrecked it, and burned his papers. "The hellish crew," said Hutchinson, "fell upon my house with the rage of devils." The disorder and confusion were so widespread that parents complained they could not get their children back to their set routines of going to school or to bed.

Following Virginia's lead, delegates from nine colonies met in a Stamp Act Congress in New York in October 1765. They petitioned the Crown against taxation without their consent and then urged the colonies to boycott British goods. Parliament backed down at the uproar and repealed the Stamp Act. But it stood by its right to tax the colonies. As long as Parliament insisted on that, trouble would not go away. The colonists were by now too experienced, too skillful, too militant to let the Crown play with their rights.

Popular protest against denial of what the colonists felt to be their rights erupted in many places. North of

New York City lay great blocks of land acquired by patronage and fraud. The Livingston family, for example, had expanded a grant of a few thousand acres into a holding of 160,000 acres—this by plain fraud when the boundaries were drawn. The lordship of such a great estate brought rich rewards. The aristocrats expected their tenants to sweat to make them even wealthier and to bow down to them when they passed. Knowing how the land had been grabbed illegally, some tenants claimed title to the farmlands they worked. The landlords called them Levellers, after the name of a popular party that sprang up during the English Revolution of the 1640s. They held all people were born free and equal, and their ideas foreshadowed many of the elements of the United States Constitution and the Bill of Rights. The tenants refused to pay their rents and, when threatened, rioted against the sheriff's deputies. By the spring of 1766 the situation grew so tense that British troops were called in. In his journal Captain John Montresor notes what happened:

APRIL 29, 1766.

The city, alarmed from the approach of the country Levellers, called the Westchester men. The militia ordered to hold themselves in readiness. Letters received from them in town declaring that if Mr. Cortlandt does not give them a grant forever to his lands, they will march with their body now collected and pull down his house in town and also one belonging to Mr. Lambert Moore.

MAY 1, 1766.

Six men (a committee from Westchester people being 500 men now lying at King's Bridge) came into town to explain matters. . . . The military applied to on account of the Levellers on which they dispersed . . .

MAY 6, 1766.

Proclamation issued 100£ reward for the taking of Pendergrast, chief of the country Levellers and 50£ for either Munro and Finch, two officers.

JUNE 28, 1766.

Advices from the Manor of Livingston that the Levellers have rose there to the number of 500 men, 200 of which had marched to murder the lord of the manor and level his house, unless he would sign leases for 'em agreeable to their form, as theirs were now expired, and that they would neither pay rent, taxes, etc., nor suffer other tenants. The Levellers met by Mr. Walter Livingston, the son, who made a sally with 40 armed men—the 200 having only sticks—obliged them to retire, not without their threatening a more respectable visit on the return of Colonel Livingston of the Manor.

JUNE 29, 1766.

Seventeen hundred of the Levellers with firearms are collected at Poughkeepsie. All the jails broke open through all the counties this side of Albany, of the east side of the river, by people headed by Pendergrast. Eight thousand cartridges sent up to the 28th Regt. . . .

ADVERTISEMENT.

THE Members of the Association of the Sons of Liberty, are requested to meet at the City-Hall, at one o'Clock, To-morrow, (being Friday) on Business of the utmost Importance;—And every other Friend to the Liberties, and Trade of America, are hereby most cordially invited, to meet at the same Time and Place. *The Committee of the Association.*

Thursday, NEW-YORK, 16th December, 1773.

The Sons of Liberty and their supporters are called to a meeting in New York. Some of the most prosperous and respectable colonials were among the leaders.

JULY 10, 1766.

This morning arrived the 28th Regiment with Pendergrast, the principal country rebel ringleader.

AUGUST 6, 1766.

Accounts from the Circuit, Pendergrast is indicted for high treason.

AUGUST 19, 1766.

Wm. Pendergrast, who was tried at Poughkeepsie and found guilty of high treason and received sentence of death, begged leave of the court to admit him to deliver a few words, viz: "That if opposition to government was deemed rebellion, no member of that court were entitled to set upon his trial."

From "Journals of Captain John Montresor, 1757–1778," New-York Historical Society, *Collections*, XIV.

7

Nothing Can Eradicate the Seeds of Liberty

From the first stirrings of rebellion through the founding of the new republic Benjamin Franklin was a great influence. He began life in 1706 as one of seventeen children of a Boston candlemaker. With less than two years of formal schooling he would gain the ear of five kings and receive the honors of six universities. So successful was he as a Philadelphia printer and tradesman that he was able to retire at forty-two—not to rest, but to continue his brilliant work as editor, statesman, diplomat, and scientist. His experiments and writings in such fields as electricity, medicine, meteorology, astronomy, magnetism, and demography, and his many practical inventions, won him great respect.

His fame was universal: "The greatest philosopher of the century," an Italian academy called him. His short Autobiography *became one of the most popular books ever published. But it was his character and personality, his wit and charm, that won him hearty affection wherever he went. He gave public service to his America for more than fifty years.*

In England, as representative of his colony of Pennsylvania and several others, Franklin helped secure the repeal of the Stamp Act. In April 1767 the wise old man

Benjamin Franklin, portrayed in pastel by J. S. Duplessis in 1783. One of the most famous men of his time, Franklin took great care to shape his public image.

sent this warning—unheeded—to one of England's political leaders, Lord Kames:

BUT AMERICA, an immense territory, favored by nature with all advantages of climate, soil, great navigable rivers

47

and lakes, etc., must become a great country, populous and mighty; and will, in a less time than is generally conceived, be able to shake off any shackles that may be imposed on her, and perhaps place them on the imposers. In the meantime, every act of oppression will sour their tempers, lessen greatly, if not annihilate, the profits of your commerce with them, and hasten their final revolt; for the seeds of liberty are universally sown there, and nothing can eradicate them.

Benjamin Franklin to Lord Kames, April 11, 1767, Abercairny
Collection, Scottish Record Office, Edinburgh.

8

A Tea Party

Resistance to the Stamp Act brought about its repeal. But other unpopular measures remained, and new ones were added. The British found how hard it is to impose authority on an unwilling people. The colonists were moving down the road from resistance to revolution. In Boston, on March 5, 1770, a crowd gathered to confront British troops guarding the customhouse. Snowballs flew in the air and the soldiers panicked. An order to fire was shouted, no one knows by whom, and five Bostonians fell dead, with many more wounded. This was the Bos-

ton Massacre. Radicals used the incident as a dramatic example of British threat to liberty and the danger of a standing army in peacetime. The soldiers involved were acquitted by a jury—packed by the Crown-appointed sheriff, it was said.

Petitions from the colonies to settle their grievances poured into London but were rejected. The colonials became convinced the entire British government—George III as well as Parliament—was ready to deny the colonists their liberties. What other measures could the colonists take?

Cool Samuel Adams was always ready with another idea. Now in his late forties, he was a great power in Massachusetts politics. He had no wealth or position, nor did he look impressive. A stout man with a nervous palsy, he lacked skill as orator or writer. But with the Stamp Act crisis he showed his great talent as one of America's first politicians. He understood the ebb and flow of public opinion and knew how to plot and promote actions that might bring about a break with Britain and lead to independence.

It was Sam Adams' idea to get the Boston town meeting to set up a Committee of Correspondence. Many other towns and colonies quickly did the same. It became a network for exchanging information and developing common action.

The network came in handy when the colonists took to boycotting British tea in protest against the duty they had to pay on it. Philadelphia and New York refused the East India Company's tea, and the ships sailed back

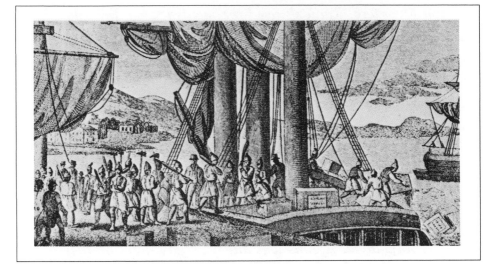

An old engraving depicts the most famous tea party in history. It was a costume party too, for many of the Bostonians disguised themselves as Mohawk Indians when they boarded the tea ships and threw 342 tea chests overboard.

to London with their cargoes. In Boston three tea ships docked at Griffin's wharf in December 1773. When the ships refused to depart with their tea, Sam Adams stood up at the town meeting and said, in a resigned voice, "This meeting can do nothing more to save the country." It was a signal. War whoops sounded from the balcony. What happened next was recalled long after by an eye-witness, Robert Sessions:

I WAS LIVING IN BOSTON at the time, in the family of a Mr. Davis, a lumber merchant, as a common laborer. On that eventful evening, when Mr. Davis came in from the town meeting, I asked him what was to be done with the tea.

"They are now throwing it overboard," he replied.

Receiving permission, I went immediately to the spot. Everything was as light as day, by the means of lamps and torches—a pin might be seen lying on the wharf. I went on board where they were at work, and took hold with my own hands.

I was not one of those appointed to destroy the tea, and who disguised themselves as Indians, but was a volunteer, the disguised men being largely men of family and position in Boston, while I was a young man whose home and relations were in Connecticut. The appointed and disguised party proving too small for the quick work necessary, other young men, similarly circumstanced with myself, joined them in their labors.

The chests were drawn up by a tackle—one man bringing them forward in the hold, another putting a rope around them, and others hoisting them to the deck and carrying them to the vessel's side. The chests were then opened, the tea emptied over the side, and the chests thrown overboard.

Perfect regularity prevailed during the whole transaction. Although there were many people on the wharf, entire silence prevailed—no clamor, no talking. Nothing was meddled with but the teas on board.

After having emptied the hold, the deck was swept clean, and everything put in its proper place. An officer on board was requested to come up from the cabin and see that no damage was done except to the tea.

From *The Night the Revolution Began*, Wesley S. Griswald, 1972.

9

You Damned Rebels

The Boston Tea Party was an act of defiance that in-furiated the British government. Coming at the end of ten years of ever-worsening relations, it brought on heavy punishment. Britain closed the port of Boston until the town would pay in full for the destroyed tea, and put Massachusetts under the control of the British army commander. The rebel colonists would be taught a les-son.

"Intolerable acts!" shouted the other colonies. They sent messages of support to Boston. Virginia proposed that they all meet to consider what to do next. In Sep-tember 1774 fifty-six delegates—a mixture of moderates and radicals—assembled in Philadelphia. They set up a Continental Association to shut off trade with Britain. In a Declaration of Rights they told Britain the colonies would no longer be bound by Parliament's laws or the king's word when it infringed on their liberties. The Congress demanded repeal of all the offensive acts passed by Parliament since 1763, and scheduled a second Con-gress for the spring of 1775.

A program bordering on revolution: It did not yet demand independence, only freedom to decide the col-onies' own affairs. It told Britain bluntly that her Amer-ican children meant to shape their own future.

The Congress knew its decisions made war possible.

If fighting was to come, the British would have to start it. Young colonials were already forming military companies and drilling with guns on the village greens. In Virginia Patrick Henry cried out to the legislature, "We must fight! Is life so dear, or peace so sweet, as to be purchased at the price of chains and slavery? Forbid it, almighty God! I know not what course others may take, but as for me, give me liberty or give me death!" The Virginians voted to prepare to fight, and asked George Washington to develop military plans.

Just then came the news some had dreaded, and many had hoped for. Blood had been spilled in Massachusetts. A British general in Boston had sent a thousand troops to capture a store of munitions at Concord hidden by farmers and village people organized as "minutemen." But an alarm had been carried to the countryside by two riders, Paul Revere and William Dawes.

Sylvanus Wood, a young shoemaker of nearby Woburn, was one of the minutemen who heard the Lexington bell tolling and felt "trouble war near." Later he recalled the historic moment:

I IMMEDIATELY AROSE, took my gun, and with Robert Douglass went in haste to Lexington. When I arrived there, I inquired of Captain Parker the news. Parker told me he did not know what to believe, for a man had come up about half an hour before and informed him that the British troops were not on the road. But while we were talking, a messenger came up and told the captain that the British troops were within half a mile. Par-

53

ker immediately turned to his drummer, and ordered him to beat to arms. . . .

The British troops approached us rapidly in platoons, with a general officer on horseback at their head. The officer came up to within about two rods of the center of the company where I stood, the first platoon being about three rods distant. There they halted. The officer then swung his sword, and said, "Lay down your arms, you damned rebels, or you are all dead men— Fire!" Some guns were fired by the British at us from the first platoon, but no person was killed or hurt, being probably charged only with powder.

Just at this time, Captain Parker ordered every man to take care of himself. The company immediately dispersed; and while the company was dispersing and leaping over the wall, the second platoon of the British fired, and killed some of our men. There was not a gun fired by any of Captain Parker's company, within my knowledge. I was so situated that I must have known it, had anything of the kind taken place before a total dispersion of our company. I have been intimately acquainted with the inhabitants of Lexington, and particularly with those of Captain Parker's company, and on one occasion, and with one exception, I have never heard any of them say or pretend that there was any firing at the British from Parker's company, or any individual in it. . . . One member of the company told me, many years since, that, after Parker's company had dispersed, and he was at some distance, he gave them "the guts of his gun."

From *Battles of the United States by Sea and Land*, Henry B. Dawson, 1858.

Amos Doolittle, himself a Minuteman, made this engraving of the Redcoats marching into Concord. At right front are British Major John Pitcairn, with spyglass, and Lieut.-Col. Francis Smith, scouting the terrain around the town cemetery.

The British troops regrouped and marched off to Concord. They entered the town without resistance and searched for military stores to destroy them. Across the Concord River minutemen had assembled. A small detail of redcoats began tearing up planks on the river bridge. Major Buttrick told his minutemen to load but not to fire unless fired upon. British guns went off, and the colonials returned the fire. There were dead and wounded on both sides. The British retreated toward town. After some costly delay they marched out, to meet the gunfire of the angry colonials whose ranks had rapidly grown.

55

In his diary British Lieutenant Frederick Mackenzie noted the way the minutemen harried the redcoats on their march back to Boston:

DURING THE WHOLE OF THE MARCH from Lexington the rebels kept an incessant irregular fire from all points at the column, which was the more galling as our flanking parties which at first were placed at sufficient distances to cover the march of it were at last, from the different obstructions they occasionally met with, obliged to keep almost close to it.

Our men had very few opportunities of getting good shots at the rebels, as they hardly ever fired but under cover of a stone wall, from behind a tree, or out of a house, and the moment they had fired, they lay down out of sight until they had loaded again or the column had passed. In the road, indeed, in our rear, they were most numerous and came on pretty close, frequently calling out "King Hancock forever!" Many of them were killed in the houses on the roadside from whence they fired; in some of them seven or eight men were destroyed. Some houses were forced open in which no person could be discovered, but when the column had passed, numbers sallied out from some place in which they had lain concealed, fired at our rear guard, and augmented the numbers which followed us.

If we had had time to set fire to those houses, many rebels must have perished in them, but as night drew on Lord Percy thought it best to continue the march. Many houses were plundered by the soldiers, notwithstanding

56

Doolittle shows British troops retreating in neat ranks down the road in the center of the engraving. In front, at the bottom, the American minutemen shoot at the enemy from behind a stone wall. The burning houses are in Lexington.

the efforts of the officers to prevent it. I have no doubt this inflamed the rebels and made many of them follow us farther than they would otherwise have done. By all accounts some soldiers who stayed too long in the houses were killed in the very act of plundering by those who lay concealed in them. We brought in about ten prisoners, some of whom were taken in arms. One or two more were killed on the march while prisoners by the fire of their own people.

Few or no women or children were to be seen throughout the day. As the country had undoubted intelligence that some troops were to march out and the rebels were probably determined to attack them, it is generally supposed they had previously removed their families from the neighborhood.

From *Diary of Frederick Mackenzie*, Frederick Mackenzie, 2 vols., 1930.

— 10 —

Against Great Odds

Express riders carrying the news of Lexington and Concord blazed through New England, down the coast to Georgia, and westward across the mountains. Weapons and powder were stored, men prepared to fight. Early in May 1775 the Second Continental Congress met in Philadelphia, with a war on its hands. Plans were laid to raise an army, funds, and supplies. As the troops of nearby colonies moved up to Boston to aid in its defense, the Congress unanimously elected George Washington to be commander in chief of a Continental army.

At forty-three, Washington was a tall, powerful man, a graceful rider, and a fine dancer. His square, handsome face was topped by fading red hair. Dignified and composed, he gave off an air of intense vitality. People

*usually felt instant confidence in him; he seemed an
unbreakable man one could always depend upon.*

*The odds were all against America. This infant nation
matching itself against the world's richest power? Against
the world's strongest army and navy? But Britain had
problems, too. She knew a war would be terribly costly,
and unpopular. Her troops were scattered around the
empire. A vast ocean lay between her and the enemy.
Sending orders and receiving reports would be agoniz-
ingly slow business.*

*How good were the troops Washington would have
to rely upon? Lord Percy, a British regimental commander, observing them in Boston, had to admire their
spirit. He wrote to London:*

WHOEVER LOOKS UPON THEM as an irregular mob will
find himself much mistaken. They have men amongst
them who know very well what they are about, having
been employed as Rangers against the Indians and Canadians; and this country, being much covered with wood
and hilly, is very advantageous for their method of fighting.

Nor are several of their men void of a spirit of en-
thusiasm, as we experienced yesterday, for many of them
concealed themselves in houses and advanced within ten
yards to fire at me and other officers, though they were
morally certain of being put to death themselves in an
instant.

You may depend upon it, that as the rebels have now
had time to prepare, they are determined to go through

with it, nor will the insurrection here turn out so de-
spicable as it is perhaps imagined at home.

From *Letters of Hugh Earl Percy, from Boston and New York,*
1774–76, Charles K. Bolton, ed., 1902.

Early in July General Washington rode into Cambridge,
close by Boston, and made it his headquarters. Looking
over his troops, he was not impressed by what he saw.
The General at once set out to mold a real fighting force.
The Reverend William Emerson of Concord visited the
army camp often and wrote his wife these impressions
of Washington's influence:

THERE IS GREAT OVERTURNING in the camp as to order and regularity. New lords, new laws. The Generals
Washington and Lee are upon the lines every day. New
orders from his Excellency are read to the respective
regiments every morning after prayers. The strictest government is taking place and great distinction is made
between officers and soldiers. Everyone is made to know
his place and keep in it, or be immediately tied up, and
receive not one but thirty or forty lashes according to
his crime. Thousands are at work every day from four
till eleven o'clock in the morning. It is surprising the
work that has been done. . . .

'Tis also very diverting to walk among the camps.
They are as different in their form as the owners are in
their dress, and every tent is a portraiture of the temper
and taste of the persons that encamp in it. Some are
made of boards, some of sailcloth, and some partly of

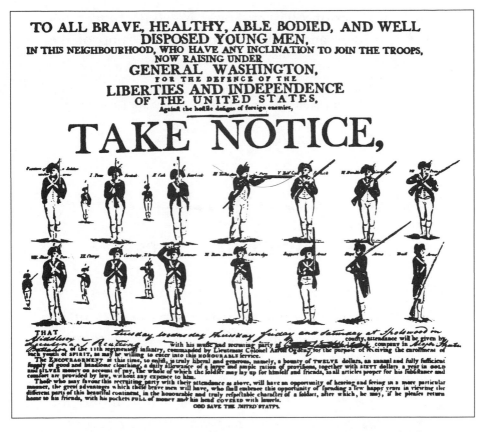

A recruiting poster issued in General Washington's name. The fine print at bottom offers a $12 bounty to join, $60 a year in pay, and "the opportunity of spending a few happy years in viewing the different parts of this beautiful continent" and returning home "with his pockets FULL of money and his head COVERED with laurels."

one and partly of the other. Others are made of stone and turf, and others again of birch and other brush. Some are thrown up in a hurry and look as if they could not help it—mere necessity—others are curiously wrought with doors and windows done with wreaths and withes

61

in the manner of a basket. Some are your proper tents and marquees and look like the regular camp of the enemy.

From "William Emerson to his wife, July 17, 1775," Bancroft Transcripts, Manuscripts Division, New York Public Library.

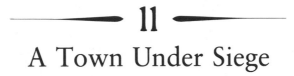

11

A Town Under Siege

Yes, the revolutionary army was a sorry enough affair to discourage any commander. With thirteen colonies jealous of their independence there was no central authority to manage the war. The Congress had to beg the colonies for troops. The colonies enlisted men only for six months' service. The soldiers chose their own officers, resisted discipline, and deserted in wholesale lots. The Congress refused to order a national draft. At last it offered money and land to men who would enlist in a Continental army for the duration. But the colonies competed by offering enlistees more to join their militias, and for shorter terms to be served in their own area.

Supply and pay for the army were just as wretchedly handled. The corruption and profiteering Washington saw sickened him. He confided his feelings to Joseph Reed in a letter of November 28, 1775:

SUCH A DEARTH OF PUBLIC SPIRIT, and want of virtue, such stock-jobbing, and fertility in all the low arts to obtain advantages of one kind or another, in this great change of military arrangement, I never saw before, and pray God I may never be witness to again. What will be the ultimate end of these maneuvers is beyond my scan. I tremble at the prospect. We have been till this time enlisting about three thousand five hundred men. To engage these I have been obliged to allow furloughs as far as fifty men a regiment, and the officers I am persuaded indulge as many more. The Connecticut troops will not be prevailed upon to stay longer than their term (saving those who have enlisted for the next campaign, and mostly on furlough), and such a dirty, mercenary spirit pervades the whole, that I should not be at all

Boston under siege of British ships. An engraving by Paul Revere.

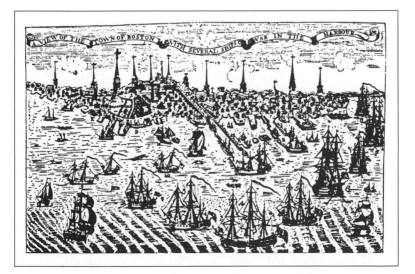

surprised at any disaster that may happen. In short, after the last of this month our lines will be so weakened that the minutemen and militia must be called in for their defense; these, being under no kind of government themselves, will destroy the little subordination I have been laboring to establish, and run me into one evil whilst I am endeavoring to avoid another; but the lesser must be chosen. Could I have foreseen what I have, and am likely to experience, no consideration upon earth should have induced me to accept this command.

From Writings of George Washington, John C. Fitzpatrick, ed., 1931–44.

But despite these troubles, the troops continued their siege of the British holed up in Boston. Although the Americans gave up Breed's Hill after three assaults by the British, they made the redcoats pay three times as much in casualties. What it was like to live in a town occupied by the British forces and under siege by American troops is conveyed in the 1775 journal of Timothy Newell of Boston:

July 14th. Last night was awoke by the discharge of cannon on the lines. Master James Lovell, Master Leach, John Hunt, have been imprisoned some time past—all they know why it is so is they are charged with free speaking on the public [British] measures; Dorrington, his son and daughter and the nurse for blowing up fires in the evening—they are charged with giving signals in this way to the army without.

July 20th. Mr. Carpenter was taken by the [British] night patrol. Upon examination he had swam over to Dorchester and back again, was tried here that day and sentence of death passed on him and to be executed the next day—his coffin brought into the jailyard, his halter bought and he dressed as criminals are before execution. Sentence was respited and a few days after was pardoned.

July 23d. The Castle, it is publicly talked, will be dismantled. This evening many guns fired at and from the [British] man of war at N. Boston. Ten or twelve transports it is said sailed this day with 150 soldiers upon a secret expedition for provisions.

August 1st. This week passed tolerably quiet. Last night at half past 12 o'clock was awoke with a heavy firing from a man of war at the [American] Provincials on Phip's farm. From the lines at Charlestown and Boston it appeared as if a general attack was made. The firing continued till 6 o'clock. The George Tavern was burnt by the Regulars and the house at the lighthouse by the Provincials (about 300) who took about 30 soldiers and a number of carpenters. This morning half past 4 o'clock awoke with cannonade and small arms from Charlestown which lasted till eleven o'clock after that.

Very trying scenes.

This day was invited by two gentlemen to dine upon rats. The whole of this day till sunset a constant fire up Mystic River from the lines and our sentinels at Charlestown and the Provincials from Mount Prospect.

August 4th. John Gill imprisoned, charged with printing sedition, treason, and rebellion.

August 16th. Cannonade from both lines.

August 17th. Cannonade again.

August 19th. Ditto. A 42-pounder split on the lines, killed a bombardier and wounded one or two men.

August 20th to 25th. Daily firing from the lines and from the sentinels on both sides.

August 27th. Sabbath. Cannonading from the lines at Charlestown on new works—a nearer approach, also much firing of small arms.

August 29th. Several bombs from ditto on ditto in the night.

August 30th. Ditto. In the night ditto. Bombarding from the lines on Bunkers Hill.

September 1st. Ditto. Almost constant firing from the sentinels at each other. New works arise upon the Neck by the Provincials who approach very near.

September 11th. A sergeant and 5 men taken by the Provincials at Dorchester.

September 12th. Went in a boat to relieve a lad blown off in a canoe.

October 17th. Two floating batteries from the Provincials from Cambridge River fired a number of cannon into the [British] camp at the common; the shot went through houses by the Lamb Tavern, etc. A deserter who came in this morning says one of the cannon split and killed and wounded several. 5 or 6 hats, a waistcoat and part of a boat came on shore at the bottom of the common.

October 25th. Several nights past the whole army was ordered not to undress. The cannon all loaded with grapeshot from a full apprehension the Provincials would make an attack upon the town. The streets paraded all night by the Light Horse.

October 27th. The spacious Old South Meeting House taken possession of by the Light Horse 17th Regiment of [British] Dragoons commanded by Lieutenant Colonel Samuel Birch. The pulpit, pews, and seats all cut to pieces and carried off in the most savage manner as can be expressed, and destined for a riding school. The beautiful carved pew with the silk furniture of Deacon Hubbard's was taken down and carried to ———'s house by an officer and made a hog sty. The above was effected by a solicitation of General Burgoyne.

October 30th. A soldier, one of the Light-Horse men, was hanged at the head of their camp for attempting to desert. Proclamation issued by [British] General Howe for the inhabitants to sign an association to take arms, etc.

November 4th. A Proclamation issued for people to give in their names to go out of town, but before the time limit expired a stop was put to it. This like others of the kind seems only designed to continue the vexation of the people.

November 9th. Several companies of regulars from Charlestown went over to Phip's farm to take a number of cattle feeding there. The Provincials came upon them and soon drove them on board boats after an engagement. It is said several are wounded and none killed, but they supposed many of the Provincials killed.

November 16th. Many people turned out of their houses for the troops to enter. The keys of our meeting house cellars demanded of me by Major Sheriff by order of General Howe. Houses, fences, trees, etc., pulled down and carried off for fuel. My wharf and barn pulled down by order of [British] General Robinson.

November 19th. A large ship arrived from Plymouth in England with every kind of provisions dead and alive, hogs, sheep, fowls, ducks, eggs, mincemeat, etc. gingerbread, etc. 25 regiments of king's troops now in this distressed town.

From "Journal of Timothy Newell," Massachusetts Historical Society Collection, 4th Series, I.

12

Did Polly Set the Sponge
for the Bread?

With a small force of volunteers, Ethan Allen and Benedict Arnold seized the British Fort Ticonderoga on Lake Champlain in May 1775 and captured cannon the Americans badly needed. Serving as regimental chaplain was Parson Smith of Sharon, Connecticut. When Mrs. Smith heard her husband was dangerously ill, she made the long and perilous journey through the wilderness to nurse him. Years later, Mrs. Smith told what life on the home front was like when war made many goods unavailable and the head of the household was away on duty. A parson's salary was only a few hundred dollars a year. On such a small sum he had not only to support his family but also to entertain strangers as well as aid the neighboring poor. In addition to his own six children, Parson Smith housed, fed, clothed, and educated an average of four penniless orphans per year. At this time there were also seven young men living in the house, studying for the ministry. In all, twenty-two persons, besides servants, were under Mrs. Smith's roof:

IN OUR PRESENT STATE of peace and plenty [1795] this does not seem so very great a burden. But, at that time, when the exactions of the mother country had rendered

69

it impossible for any but the wealthiest to import anything to eat or wear, and all had to be raised and manufactured at home, from bread stuffs, sugar, and rum to the linen and woolen for our clothes and bedding, you may well imagine that my duties were not light. Though I can say for myself that I never complained, even in my inmost thoughts, for if I could even give up, for the honored cause of liberty, the husband whom I loved so dearly that my constant fear was lest I should sin to idolatry, it would assuredly have ill become me to repine at any inconvenience to myself.

And besides, to tell the truth, I had no leisure for murmuring. I rose with the sun and all through the long day I had no time for aught but my work. So much did it press upon me that I could scarcely divert my thoughts from its demands, even during the family prayers, which thing both amazed and displeased me, for during that hour, at least, I should have been sending all my thoughts to heaven for the safety of my beloved husband and the salvation of our hapless country. Instead of which I was often wondering whether Polly had remembered to set the sponge for the bread, or to put water on the leach tub, or to turn the cloth in the dying vat, or whether wool had been carded for Betsey to start her spinning wheel in the morning, or Billy had chopped light wood enough for the kindling, or dry hard wood enough to heat the big oven, or whether some other thing had not been forgotten of the thousand that must be done without fail, or else there would be a disagreeable hitch in the housekeeping.

So you may be sure that when I went to bed at night,

Whether husbands like Pastor Smith were at home or away, women worked hard raising the family, caring for guests or boarders, keeping the house, and doing the chores indoors and out.

I went to sleep, and not to lie awake imagining all sorts of disasters that might happen. There was generally enough that had happened to keep my mind at work if I stayed awake, but that I very seldom did. A perfectly healthy woman has good powers of sleep. . . .

On the third Sabbath in September Dr. Bellamy gave us a sound and clear sermon in which God's watchful providence over his people was most beautifully depicted and drew tears from the eyes of those who were unused to weeping. . . . On that night I went to bed in a calmer and more contented frame of mind than usual. I had, to be sure, been much displeased to find that our supply of bread (through some wasteful mismanagement of Polly's) had grown so small that the baking would have to be done on Monday morning, which is not good house-keeping; for the washing should always be done on Monday and the bakings on Tuesday, Thursday, and Saturday. But I had caused Polly to set a large sponge and made Billy provide plenty of firing, so that by getting up betimes in the morning, we could have the brick oven heated and the baking out of the way by the time Billy and Jack should have gotten the clothes pounded out ready for boiling, so that the two things should not interfere with each other. The last thought on my mind after committing my dear husband and country into our maker's care for the night, was to charge my mind to rise even before daylight that I might be able to execute my plans. . . .

As early as three o'clock in the morning I called Nancy and Judy, Jack, and young Billy, but would not allow old Billy to be disturbed; whereat the rest marveled, seeing that I was not used to be more tender of him than of any of the other servants, but rather the less so in that he was my own slave that my father had given to me upon my marriage. But I let them marvel, for truly it was no concern of theirs, and by five o'clock the bread was ready to be molded, the hickory coals were lying in a great glowing mass on the oven bottom, casting a brilliant light over its vaulted top and sending such a heat into my face when I passed by the oven mouth that it caused me to think then, as it always does, of Neb-uchadnezzar's fiery furnace, seven times heated.

Young Billy was already pounding out the clothes, and over the fire Jack was hanging the great brass kettles for the wash, while Nancy and Judy had made ready the smoking hot piles of Johnnycake, the boiler of wheat coffee (which was all we could get in those days, and a poor substitute it was for good mocha) and the big platter of ham and eggs and plenty of good potatoes roasted in the ashes, which is the best way that potatoes can be cooked, in my opinion.

From *Colonial Days and Ways*, Helen E. Smith, 1900.

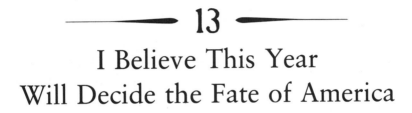

13

I Believe This Year
Will Decide the Fate of America

Josiah Bartlett of Kingston, New Hampshire, was a country doctor and farmer committed to science and reason and concerned to raise the practise of medicine to a recognized profession. Early on he opposed British domination of the colonies and organized against it. He was elected a member of the Continental Congress. When he was busy at its sessions in Philadelphia or New York, he and his wife Mary exchanged letters that reveal their affectionate concern for one another in the long periods of loneliness and their interests and activities during the

Revolutionary War. Bartlett, the son of a shoemaker, was a signer of the Declaration of Independence and helped write the new nation's Constitution. Later he became Governor of New Hampshire. These are not all the letters they wrote. Some may be missing, as in the gap between 1776 and 1778:

From Josiah

PHILADELPHIA, JULY 2, 1776.

Rode 6 miles to Germantown before breakfast. . . . Went to see the British Museum, so called. It is a house built on purpose to preserve all the natural curiosities that can be collected from all parts of the world, as birds, beasts, fish shells, snakes, plants, and a great many other curiosities. Among them there was a shark, a crocodile, a catfish, a dogfish, a sea porcupine, a creature called a hog in armor, 2 ostrich's eggs, which were perfectly round and of the color of ivory and, I guess, would hold a pint and a half each. There was a great many other creatures of a strange make from anything I ever saw before. . . .

UNDATED

Other curiosities: two or three tons of ice. They use it to cool their liquors in the summer, particularly punch; fresh meat laid on it will keep a week in the hottest weather. Another curiosity was two fish pools for breeding fish. . . .

From shoemaker's son to Governor of New Hampshire was the course his role in the American Revolution made possible for Dr. Josiah Bartlett.

PHILADELPHIA, SEPTEMBER 9, 1776.

Hasty pudding is here called mush.

PHILADELPHIA, JUNE 17, 1776.

The affair of a Confederation of the colonies, independence, etc., is now on the carpet and will soon be published, I expect. Remember my love to all my children, in particular.

From Mary

I hope we all shall be kept in health, peace and safety. We have the same keeper though we are separated, yet God is everywhere present. A general time of health. We have had a great plenty of rain this week.

I am in great hopes the English corn will be very good this year. Indian corn grows very fast. I believe hay will be better than our fears; in short, these bountiful rains have revived the face of the earth. . . . We have had very sharp lightning and heavy thunder which has struck trees and the grounds several times. As the weather is much hotter with you than with us I shall be glad to know whether you have heavy thunder and lightning there or no.

KINGSTON, JULY 13 and 15, 1776.

Our people met here for training and town meetings three days this week to list men to go to Canada. . . . Old Mr. Proctor and Old Will Collins of this town and several younger men have enlisted. They are to march next week, I hear. I want your advice and assistance but must make myself contented. . . . Peter is more steady now than he was when you left him before.

P.S. I fear the smallpox will spread universally as Boston is shut up with it and people flocking in for inoculation. . . . The times look dark and gloomy upon the account of the wars. I believe this year will decide the fate of America—which way it will turn God only knows. We must look to Him for direction and protection; Job said though He slay me yet will I trust in Him. *July 15.* We are all well.

KINGSTON, JULY 20, 1776.

Ezra was taken last Monday in the afternoon (after we had dated a letter to you that we were well) with the canker and scarlet fever. He is now some better. The men among us are very backward about going into the war. They are not contented with the province bounty. Our men have had a town meeting and have voted to raise their bounty to fifty dollars a man besides their wages. They are to begin their march today and meet at Esq. Webster's at Chester. David Quimby of Hawk is captain, John Eastman second lieutenant, Old Mr. Proctor is gone, Mr. Wheeler is a-going.

KINGSTON, JULY 29, 1776.

There has been no funeral in this parish since them I mentioned you, but in the East Parish Mrs. Tilton, wife of Captain Tilton, buried her only daughter last Wednesday. About four or five years old, she died with the fever and canker. He is gone to Canada—heavy news to him when he comes to hear of it.

KINGSTON, AUGUST 9, 1776.

John Noyes says he has been in England, and several of the West Indies islands. But he says America is the only

77

place for living comfortably, if we can enjoy our liberty. He says some of the people in England is almost as stupid as the brute creation; they are so ignorant they could hardly believe he was an American because, they said, he looked and spoke so much like an Englishman.

The people among us is very hurried getting in the harvest. I believe they will chiefly finish this week. We have cut all our grain; something late getting in hay. We have not half done as the grass grew very fast of late. Plenty of rains; the weather not very hot.

KINGSTON, AUGUST 29, 1776.

Prices of things have been extravagant—molasses four and six pence per gallon . . . New England rum five shillings per gallon, West India seven and six pence per gallon, cotton wool four shillings per pound, Bohea tea ten shillings per pound, and other things in proportion. Men's days work some three shillings and some four shillings per day.

KINGSTON, SEPTEMBER 9, 1776.

Help is so scarce we could not get one days work about reaping upon any account and one about mowing. But what I paid the money for we have almost done haying. . . . Our English corn is not threshed yet. Apples scarce, plums in the garden plenty. Pray do come home before cold weather, as you know my circumstances will be difficult in the winter, if I am alive.

From Josiah

Remember my love to all my children. I want to know how hay is likely to be with us; how the English corn is like to be; whether the worms destroy the Indian corn; how the flax is like to turn out, etc. etc. Remember me to David Sanborn and tell him I feel pretty easy about my farming affairs as long as I know he has the care of it.

PHILADELPHIA, AUGUST 24, 1778.

I am sorry to hear there is like to be a scarcity of cider, as I sensibly feel the want of it here, where there is always a scarcity or rather where they never use much of it, and what is made is very inferior to the New England cider. If I am not likely to make any I hope you will purchase a few barrels as I should be glad of a little (after so long fasting from it) when I return home. . . .

The little bobbed hats for the men are growing fast out of fashion. The mode now is large round brims and cocked nearly three square. No hats are now made in any other mode here. So much for fashions, for the satisfaction of my children. . . .

From *The Old Revolutionaries*, Pauline Maier, 1980.

14

'Tis Time to Part

As the siege of Boston dragged into the winter of 1775–76, some Americans began to turn toward independence, toward a complete break with the mother country. King George III was no longer the court of final appeal. By his harsh measures against the colonies, by the acts of Parliament and the king's ministers, it was plain that Britain had no sense of how to govern America. The Continental Congress, struggling with the problems of conducting a war, was really a government in action. But it had not yet found the will to break with Britain.

Then, on January 9, 1776, a political bombshell exploded. It was a pamphlet—Thomas Paine's Common Sense. *A poor English immigrant looking for a new start in life, Paine had settled in Philadelphia less than two years before. Siding with the radicals, he argued that "everything that is right or natural pleads for separation. The blood of the slain, the weeping voice of nature cries,* 'TIS TIME TO PART."

His appeal for immediate independence quickly sold 150,000 copies, a huge number at a time when the most popular newspapers sold about two thousand copies per week. Paine's savage attack on England made brilliantly clear to Americans what they were against—the British system itself, with its monarchy and its inequality. He called not only for independence, but also for the establishment of a republic—a representative form of government.

Paine's ideas were not original. What was new was the way he combined them into a single powerful argument, and his clear, direct style meant to bring his message to the widest possible audience. He believed anyone could understand what politics and government were about. Don't look to authority, he said: rely on "nothing more than the simple facts, plain argument, and common sense." He was a fine literary craftsman who carefully wrote and rewrote to attain the effects he wanted.

Here are some of the important arguments Paine made:

ALAS! We have been long led away by ancient prejudices and made large sacrifices to superstition. We have boasted the protection of Great Britain, without considering that her motive was interest, not attachment, and that she did not protect us from our enemies on our account, but from her enemies on her own account. . . .

But Britain is the parent country say some. Then the more shame upon her conduct. Even brutes do not devour their young, nor savages make war upon their families. . . . Europe and not England is the parent country of America. This New World has been the asylum for the persecuted lovers of civil and religious liberty from every part of Europe. Hither have they fled, not from the tender embraces of the mother, but from the cruelty

COMMON SENSE,

ADDRESSED TO THE

INHABITANTS

OF

AMERICA,

On the following interesting

SUBJECTS.

I. Of the Origin and Design of Government in general,
with concise Remarks on the English Constitution.

II. Of Monarchy and Hereditary Succession.

III. Thoughts on the present State of American Affairs.

IV. Of the present Ability of America, with some mis-
cellaneous Reflections.

Man knows no Master save creating HEAVEN,
Or those whom choice and common good ordain.
THOMSON.

PHILADELPHIA;
Printed, and Sold, by R. BELL, in Third-Street.
MDCCLXXVI.

The cover of the original two-shilling pamphlet by Thomas Paine that called for an immediate separation from Britain. "Sound and reasonable" was the response of George Washington and innumerable others. Paine's portrait, at right, is by John Wesley Jarvis, a leading artist of that day.

of the monster; and it is so far true of England that the same tyranny which drove the first emigrants from home pursues their descendants still. . . .

It is not in the power of Britain to do this continent justice; the business of it will soon be too weighty and intricate to be managed with any tolerable degree of convenience, by a power so distant from us, and so very ignorant of us; for if they cannot conquer us, they cannot govern us. To be always running three or four thousand miles with a tale or a petition, waiting four or five months for an answer, which when obtained requires five or six more to explain it in, will in a few years be looked upon as folly and childishness—There was a time when it was proper, and there is a proper time for it to cease. . . .

America is only a secondary object in the system of

British politics. England consults the good of this country no further than it answers her own purpose. Wherefore, her own interest leads her to suppress the growth of ours in every case which doth not promote her advantage, or in the least interferes with it. . . .

It is unreasonable to suppose that France or Spain will give us any kind of assistance, if we mean only to make use of that assistance for the purpose of repairing the breach and strengthening the connection between Britain and America; because, those powers would be sufferers by the consequences.

While we profess ourselves the subjects of Britain, we must, in the eyes of foreign nations, be considered as Rebels. . . .

Were a manifest to be published and despatched to foreign courts, setting forth the miseries we have endured, and the peaceful methods which we have ineffectually used for redress . . . at the same time, assuring all such courts of our peaceable disposition toward them, and of our desire of entering into trade with them; such a memorial would produce more good effects to this continent than if a ship were freighted with petitions to Britain.

From Common Sense, Thomas Paine, 1776.

— 15 —

Remember the Ladies!

Many American women were devoted to the revolutionary movement. When colonials were urged to apply economic pressure on Britain by boycotting her products, women banded together to carry it out. In Boston, in 1770, three hundred "ladies of the highest rank and influence" pledged themselves not to use tea:

AT A TIME when our invaluable rights and privileges are attacked in an unconstitutional and most alarming manner, and as we find we are reproached for not being so ready as could be desired to lend our assistance, we think it our duty perfectly to concur with the true friends of liberty, in all the measures they have taken to save this abused country from ruin and slavery. And particularly we join with the very respectable body of merchants and other inhabitants of this town . . . in their resolutions, totally to abstain from the use of TEA. And, as the greatest part of the revenue arising [from the latest acts from England] is produced from the duty paid on tea—we the subscribers do strictly [agree] that we will totally abstain from the use of [tea](sickness excepted), not only in our respective families, but that we will absolutely

Abigail Adams, with no formal schooling, eagerly gathered knowl-edge from her wide reading of literature and history. She married John Adams and freely spoke her mind on public issues, to him and many others. Her superb letters are a great source of infor-mation about the life of her generation.

refuse it, if it should be offered to us upon any occasion whatsoever. . . .

From the *Boston Evening Post*, February 12, 1770.

With goods in ever shorter supply as the war went on, some merchants seized the chance to profiteer at the citizens' expense. Abigail Adams, in a letter to her hus-band John, away at the Continental Congress, describes the action taken by the Boston women:

I HAVE NOTHING NEW to entertain you with, unless it be an account of a new set of nobility, which has lately taken the lead in Boston. You must know that there is a great scarcity of sugar and coffee, articles which the female part of the state is very loath to give up, especially whilst they consider the scarcity occasioned by the merchants having secreted a large quantity. There had been much rout and noise in town for several weeks. Some stores had been opened by a number of people, and the coffee and sugar carried into the market and dealt out by pounds.

It is rumored that an eminent, wealthy, stingy merchant [Thomas Boylston] (also a bachelor) had a hogshead of coffee in his store, which he refused to sell to the committee under six shillings per pound. A number of females—some say a hundred, some say more—assembled with a cart and trucks, marched down to the warehouse and demanded the keys, which he refused to deliver. Upon which one of them seized him by his neck, and tossed him into the cart. Upon his finding no quarter, he delivered the keys, when they tipped up the cart and discharged him, then opened up the warehouse, hoisted out the coffee themselves, put it into the trucks and drove off.

The correspondence between John and Abigail Adams provides insight into an extraordinary relationship. Abigail was as aware of political events and ideas as any of the revolutionary leaders. But she could not be more than an observer and supporter of her husband's polit-

ical career. Many established ideas and institutions were under attack then, but not the traditional one that shut women out of public life. The private world of the family was held to be their sphere. They did not vote, hold office, or even attend town meetings. So wives and daughters exerted political influence only through their relationships to men. The highly talented Abigail Adams did just that, helping to shape the political views of her husband. These excerpts from their letters are famous for those ringing words, "Remember the Ladies!":

Abigail to John

2 MARCH 1776.

I was greatly rejoiced at the return of your servant, to find you had safely arrived [in Philadelphia], and that you were well. . . . I am charmed with the sentiments of *Common Sense*, and wonder how an honest heart, one who wishes the welfare of his country and the happiness of posterity, can hesitate one moment at adopting them. I want to know how these sentiments are received in Congress. I dare say there would be no difficulty in procuring a vote and instructions from all the assemblies in New England for independence. I most sincerely wish that now, in the lucky moment [before war], it might be done.

MARCH 31, 1776.

I long to hear that you have declared an independency— and, by the way, in the new code of laws, which I suppose it will be necessary for you to make, I desire you would remember the ladies, and be more generous and favorable to them than [were] your ancestors. Do not put such unlimited power into the hands of the husbands. Remember all men would be tyrants if they could. If particular care and attention is not paid to the ladies, we are determined to [instigate] a rebellion, and will not hold ourselves bound by any laws in which we have no voice or representation.

That your sex are naturally tyrannical is a truth so thoroughly established as to admit of no dispute. But such of you as wish to be happy willingly give up the harsh title of master for the more tender and endearing one of friend. Why, then, not put it out of the power of the vicious and the lawless to use us with cruelty and indignity . . . ? Men of sense in all ages abhor those customs which treat us only as the vassals of your sex. Regard us then as beings, placed by providence under your protection, and in imitation of the Supreme Being make use of that power only for our happiness.

John to Abigail

APRIL 14, 1776.

As to your extraordinary code of laws, I cannot but laugh. We have been told that our struggle has loosened the bands of government everywhere. That children and apprentices were disobedient—that schools and colleges were grown turbulent—that Indians slighted their guardians and Negroes grew insolent to their masters. But your letter was the first intimation that another tribe more numerous and powerful than all the rest [had]

John Adams, a short, stubby, irritable man whose ideas and leadership were of great value to the Revolution.

grown discontented. This is rather too coarse a compliment, but you are so saucy, I won't blot it out.

Depend upon it, we know better than to repeal our masculine systems. Although they are in full force, you know they are little more than theory. We dare not exert our power in its full latitude. We are obliged to go fair and softly, and, in practice, you know, we are the subjects. We have only the name of masters, and rather than give up this, which would completely subject us to the despotism of the petticoat, I hope General Washington, and all our brave heroes would fight. . . . A fine story, indeed. I begin to think the ministry as deep as they are wicked. After stirring up Tories, landjobbers, trimmers, bigots, Canadians, Indians, Negroes, Hanoverians, Hessians, Russians, Irish Roman Catholics, Scotch . . . at last they have stimulated the [women] to demand new privileges and [to] threaten to rebel.

Abigail to John

MAY 7, 1776.

I cannot say that I think you very generous to the ladies. For, whilst you are proclaiming peace and good will to men, emancipating all nations, you insist upon retaining an absolute power over wives. But you must remember that arbitrary power is like most other things which are very hard—very liable to be broken; and, notwithstanding all your wise laws and maxims, we have it in our power not only to free ourselves but to subdue our masters, and without violence throw both your natural and legal authority at our feet.

From *Familiar Letters of John Adams and His Wife Abigail Adams, During the Revolution*, Charles Francis Adams, ed., 1876.

— 16 —

We Hold These Truths

Reading Common Sense *in camp, General Washington declared it "sound doctrine and unanswerable reason." His letters urged influential friends to push for independence. In March 1776 the British shipped out of Boston, taking about a thousand loyalists with them. By May the Continental Congress was using the term "states," not "colonies," and advising the states to establish governments independent of Britain. On June 7th a Virginia delegate introduced an independence resolution in Congress. The delegates debated it for several days, meanwhile appointing a committee to draft a declaration of independence, just in case. On July 2, the Congress resolved "that these United Colonies are, and of right, ought to be free and independent states."*

It was Thomas Jefferson of Virginia, only thirty-three, who was asked to draft the Declaration of Independence with the helping hands of committee members Benjamin Franklin and John Adams. Jefferson was tall, slender, and red-haired. His shyness made him seem stiff to strangers. He was a brilliant student with an extraordinary range of interest and skills in the arts and sciences. A competent lawyer, he served in the Virginian legislature and the Continental Congress. At this time he was a rising star in Virginia's ruling class. Congress made some further changes in Jefferson's draft, taking out most importantly an attack upon the slave trade, for which the king had been blamed. This deletion was made, said Jefferson at the time, upon the request of South Carolina and Georgia, "who had never attempted to restrain the importation of slaves, and who on the contrary still wished to continue it. Our northern brethren also I believe felt a little tender under those censures, for though their people had very few slaves themselves yet they had been pretty considerable carriers of them to others."

On July fourth the Declaration was adopted, and then printed. The text was read aloud to jubilant crowds throughout the states. A year later the country began the now hallowed tradition of celebrating the Fourth of July as Independence Day.

The aim of the Declaration, Jefferson wrote later, was not to say something new. Rather, it was "to place before mankind the common sense of the subject, in terms so plain and firm as to command their assent. . . . Neither aiming at originality of principles nor sentiments, nor yet copied from any particular and previous writing, it was intended to be an expression of the American mind."

The Declaration has a preamble stating the rights at issue, followed by a list of grievances about the infringements upon those rights, and it closes with a mutual pledge to support the steps taken to independence. Here is the text, minus the specific charges against Britain and the king:

WHEN IN THE COURSE of human events, it becomes necessary for one people to dissolve the political bands which have connected them with another, and to assume among the powers of the earth, the separate and equal station to which the laws of nature and of nature's God entitle them, a decent respect to the opinions of mankind requires that they should declare the causes which impel them to the separation.

We hold these truths to be self-evident, that all men are created equal, that they are endowed by their Creator with certain unalienable rights, that among these are life, liberty, and the pursuit of happiness.

That to secure these rights, governments are instituted among men, deriving their just powers from the consent of the governed, that whenever any form of government becomes destructive of these ends, it is the right of the people to alter or to abolish it, and to institute new government, laying its foundation on such principles and organizing its powers in such form, as to them shall seem most likely to effect their safety and happiness. Prudence, indeed, will dictate that governments long established should not be changed for light and transient causes; and accordingly, all experience hath shown, that mankind are more disposed to suffer, while evils are sufferable, than to right themselves by abolishing the forms to which they are accustomed. But when a long train of abuses and usurpations, pursuing invariably the same object evinces a design to reduce them under absolute despotism, it is their right, it is their duty, to throw off such government, and to provide new guards for their future security.

The committee to draw up a Declaration of Independence presents it to the Second Continental Congress in Philadelphia in 1776. In rear center is Thomas Jefferson, handing the draft to John Hancock, seated in the back. Seated in front center is Benjamin Franklin. Standing at left center of the group is John Adams.

Such has been the patient sufferance of these colonies; and such is now the necessity which constrains them to alter their former systems of government. The history of the present king of Great Britain is a history of repeated injuries and usurpations, all having in direct object the establishment of an absolute tyranny over these states. To prove this, let facts be submitted to a candid world. . . .

We, therefore, the representatives of the United States of America, in General Congress, Assembled, appealing to the Supreme Judge of the world for the rectitude of our intentions, do, in the name and by authority of the good people of these colonies, solemnly publish and declare, that these united colonies are, and of right ought to be free and independent states; that they are absolved from all allegiance to the British Crown, and that all political connection between them and the state of Great Britain, is and ought to be totally dissolved; and that as free and independent states, they have full power to levy war, conclude peace, contract alliances, establish commerce, and to do all other acts and things which independent states may of right do. And for the support of this declaration, with a firm reliance on the protection of Divine Providence, we mutually pledge to each other our lives, our fortunes and our sacred honor.

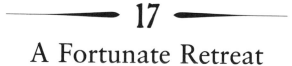

17

A Fortunate Retreat

Remember, when the Declaration of Independence was adopted, the colonies were already governing themselves. The Declaration was a formal recognition of that fact. A major motive for the Declaration was to make it easier to secure foreign help in the war against Britain. General Washington badly needed supplies and more money and manpower if he was to have any chance to win. Now, with legal standing as a nation, negotiations began for a treaty with France, a power that badly wanted to see its old enemy, Britain, defeated.

In that same summer of 1776 the Congress put a committee to work drafting a permanent frame of government, the Articles of Confederation. Some terms of alliance were needed to bind the thirteen separate states into a nation. As the Articles were not ratified by the states until 1781, most of the war would be conducted by the Congress.

Meanwhile, the war went on. In August of 1776 a British fleet of two hundred ships landed thirty thousand troops on the western tip of Long Island, where Brooklyn is now. In the Battle of Long Island that followed, the superior British forces defeated Washington's army, and might have destroyed it if the General had not staged a masterly retreat on the night of August 29. Here Colonel Benjamin Tallmadge of Connecticut recalls that dreadful night:

THIS WAS THE FIRST time in my life that I had witnessed the awful scene of a battle when man was engaged to destroy his fellowman. I well remember my sensations on the occasion, for they were solemn beyond description, and very hardly could I bring my mind to be willing to attempt the life of a fellow creature. Our army having retired behind their entrenchment . . . the British army took their position in full array, directly in front of our position. Our entrenchment was so weak that it is most wonderful the British general did not attempt to storm it soon after the battle in which his troops had been victorious.

General Washington was so fully aware of the perilous situation of this division of his army that he immediately convened a council of war, at which the propriety of retiring to New York was decided on. After sustaining incessant fatigue and constant watchfulness for two days and nights, attended by heavy rain, exposed every moment to an attack from a vastly superior force in front, and to be cut off from the possibility of a retreat to New York by the fleet which might enter the East River, on the night of the 29th of August General Washington commenced recrossing his troops from Brooklyn to New York.

To move so large a body of troops, with all their necessary appendages, across a river a full mile wide, with a rapid current, in the face of a victorious, well-disciplined army nearly three times as numerous as his own, and a fleet capable of stopping the navigation so that not one boat could have passed over, seemed to present most formidable obstacles. But in face of these difficulties, the commander in chief so arranged his business that on the evening of the 29th, by 10 o'clock, the troops began to retire from the lines in such a manner that no chasm was made in the lines but as one regiment left their station on guard, the remaining troops moved to the right and left and filled up the vacancies, while General Washington took his station at the ferry and superintended the embarkation of the troops.

It was one of the most anxious, busy nights that I

Washington's troops retreating under British fire in the Battle of Long Island.

ever recollect, and being the third in which hardly any of us had closed our eyes in sleep, we were all greatly fatigued. As the dawn of the next day approached, those of us who remained in the trenches became very anxious for our own safety, and when the dawn appeared there were several regiments still on duty. At this time a very dense fog began to rise, and it seemed to settle in a peculiar manner over both encampments. I recollect this peculiar providential occurrence perfectly well; and so very dense was the atmosphere that I could scarcely discern a man at six yards' distance.

When the sun rose we had just received orders to leave the lines, but before we reached the ferry, the commander in chief sent one of his aides to order the regiment to repair again to their former station on the lines. Colonel Chester immediately faced to the right about and returned, where we tarried until the sun had risen, but the fog remained as dense as ever. Finally, the second order arrived for the regiment to retire, and we very joyfully bid those trenches a long adieu. When we reached Brooklyn ferry, the boats had not returned from their last trip, but they very soon appeared and took the whole regiment over to New York; and I think I saw General Washington on the ferry stairs when I stepped into one of the last boats that received the troops. I left my horse tied to a post at the ferry.

The troops having now all safely reached New York, and the fog continuing as thick as ever, I began to think of my favorite horse and requested leave of volunteers to go with me, and guiding the boat myself, I obtained my horse and got off some distance into the river before the enemy appeared in Brooklyn.

As soon as they reached the ferry we were saluted merrily from their musketry, and finally by their field pieces; but we returned in safety. In the history of warfare I do not recollect a more fortunate retreat. After all, the providential appearance of the fog saved a part of our army from being captured, and certainly myself, among others who formed the rear guard. General Washington has never received the credit which was due to him for this wise and most fortunate measure.

From *Memoir of Col. Benj. Tallmadge*, Benjamin Tallmadge, 1858.

18

We Pounced Upon the Hessians Like an Eagle

The British followed Washington across the East River, up Manhattan Island, over to the Jersey shore, and then on to the Delaware River. (New York City would remain under British occupation until the war's end.) So weak were his forces that Washington chose to retreat and retreat, rather than risk the wiping out of his army. It had shrunk to 3,000 men, half its size before the campaign began. Volunteers had completed their short terms and packed off for home. Many others deserted, and the fresh militia Washington expected did not show up.

But the General decided nevertheless to strike back at the British on Christmas night, 1776, by a dangerous crossing of the Delaware into New Jersey to surprise the Hessian troops celebrating the holiday in Trenton. King George III, short of soldiers, had managed to hire thirty thousand troops from Hesse and other German principalities.

Just before the crossing of the Delaware, Tom Paine had written The American Crisis, *"in a passion of patriotism," as he put it. Washington ordered the ringing words to be read aloud to the troops as they prepared for the fight:*

THESE ARE THE TIMES that try men's souls. The summer soldier and the sunshine patriot will, in this crisis, shrink from the service of their country; but he that stands it *now*, deserves the love and thanks of man and woman.

One of Washington's aides, young Colonel John Fitzgerald, recorded how Trenton was taken:

DECEMBER 25, CHRISTMAS MORNING. They make a great deal of Christmas in Germany, and no doubt the Hessians will drink a great deal of beer and have a dance tonight. They will be sleepy tomorrow morning. Washington will set the tune for them about daybreak. The rations are cooked. New flints and ammunition have been distributed. Colonel Glover's fishermen from Marblehead, Massachusetts, are to manage the boats just as they did in the retreat from Long Island.

CHRISTMAS, 6 P.M. The regiments have had their evening parade, but instead of returning to their quarters are marching toward the ferry. It is fearfully cold and raw, and a snowstorm setting in. The wind is northeast and beats in the faces of the men. It will be a terrible night for the soldiers who have no shoes. Some of them have tied old rags around their feet; others are barefoot, but I have not heard a man complain. They are ready to suffer any hardship and die rather than give up their liberty. I have just copied the order for marching. Both divisions are to go from the ferry to Bear Tavern, two miles. They will separate there; Washington will accompany Greene's division with a part of the artillery down the Pennington road. Sullivan and the rest of the artillery will take the river road.

December 26, 3 a.m.   I am writing in the ferry house. The troops are all over, and the boats have gone back for the artillery. We are three hours behind the set time. Glover's men have had a hard time to force the boats through the floating ice with the snow drifting in their faces. I never have seen Washington so determined as he is now. He stands on the bank of the river, wrapped in his cloak, superintending the landing of his troops. He is calm and collected, but very determined. The storm is changing to sleet and cuts like a knife. The last cannon is being landed, and we are ready to mount our horses.

December 26, Noon.   It was nearly four o'clock when we started. The two divisions divided at Bear Tavern. At Birmingham, three and a half miles south of the tavern, a man came with a message from General Sullivan that the storm was wetting the muskets and rendering them unfit for service.

"Tell General Sullivan," said Washington, "to use the bayonet. I am resolved to take Trenton."

It was broad daylight when we came to a house where a man was chopping wood. He was very much surprised when he saw us.

"Can you tell me where the Hessian picket is?" Washington asked.

The man hesitated, but I said, "You need not be fright-

103

ened, it is General Washington who asks the question."

His face brightened, and he pointed toward the house of Mr. Howell.

It was just eight o'clock. Looking down the road I saw a Hessian running out of the house. He yelled in Dutch and swung his arms. Three or four others came out with their guns. Two of them fired at us, but the bullets whistled over our heads. Some of General Stephen's men rushed forward and captured two. The others took to their heels, running toward Mr. Calhoun's house, where the picket guard was stationed, about twenty men under Captain Altenbrockum. They came running out of the house. The captain flourished his sword and tried to form his men. Some of them fired at us, others ran toward the village.

The next moment we heard drums beat and a bugle sound, and then from the west came the boom of a cannon. General Washington's face lighted up instantly, for he knew that it was one of Sullivan's guns.

We could see a great commotion down toward the meetinghouse, men running here and there, officers swinging their swords, artillerymen harnessing their horses. Captain Forrest unlimbered his guns. Washington gave the order to advance, and we rushed on to the junction of King and Queen streets. Forrest wheeled six of his cannon into position to sweep both streets. The riflemen under Colonel Hand and Scott's and Lawson's battalions went upon the run through the fields on the left to gain possession of the Princeton Road. The Hessians were just ready to open fire with two of their

The day after Christmas, 1776, the Americans surprise Hessian mercenaries and win the Battle of Trenton. A lithograph made to celebrate the Centennial in 1876.

cannon when Captain [William] Washington and Lieutenant [James] Monroe with their men rushed forward and captured them.

We saw Rall coming riding up the street from his headquarters, which were at Stacy Potts' house. We could hear him shouting in Dutch, "My brave soldiers, advance!"

His men were frightened and confused, for our men were firing upon them from fences and houses and they were falling fast. Instead of advancing they ran into an apple orchard. The officers tried to rally them, but our men kept advancing and picking off the officers. It was not long before Rall tumbled from his horse and his soldiers threw down their guns and gave themselves up as prisoners.

While this was taking place on the Pennington road, Colonel John Stark from New Hampshire, in the advance on the river road, was driving Knyphausen's men pell-mell through the town. Sullivan sent a portion of his troops under St. Clair to seize the bridge and cut off the retreat of the Hessians toward Bordentown. Sullivan's men shot the artillery horses and captured two cannon attached to Knyphausen's regiment.

DECEMBER 26, 3 P.M.   I have been talking with Rall's adjutant, Lieutenant Piel. He says that Rall sat down to a grand dinner at the Trenton Tavern Christmas Day, that he drank a great deal of wine and sat up nearly all night playing cards. He had been in bed for a short time when the battle began and was sound asleep. Piel shook him, but found it hard work to wake him up. Supposing he was wide awake, Piel went out to help rally the men, but Rall not appearing, he went back and found him in his nightshirt.

"What's the matter?" Rall asked.

Piel informed him that a battle was going on. That seemed to bring him to his senses. He dressed himself, rushed out, and mounted his horse to be mortally wounded a few minutes later.

We have taken nearly one thousand prisoners, six cannon, more than one thousand muskets, twelve drums, and four colors. About forty Hessians were killed or wounded. Our loss is only two killed and three wounded.

Cartoon of a Hessian grenadier, made in 1778.

Two of the latter are Captain [William] Washington and Lieutenant [James] Monroe, who rushed forward very bravely to seize the cannon.

I have just been with General Washington and Greene to see Rall. He will not live through the night. He asked that his men might be kindly treated. Washington promised that he would see they were well cared for.

DECEMBER 27, 1776. Here we are back in our camp with the prisoners and trophies. Washington is keeping his promise; the soldiers are in the Newtown Meeting House and other buildings. He has just given directions for tomorrow's dinner. All the captured Hessian officers are to dine with him. He bears the Hessians no malice, but says they have been sold by their Grand Duke to King George and sent to America, when if they could have their own way, they would be peaceably living in their own country.

It is a glorious victory. It will rejoice the hearts of our friends everywhere and give new life to our hitherto waning fortunes. Washington has baffled the enemy in his retreat from New York. He has pounced upon the Hessians like an eagle upon a hen and is safe once more on this side of the river. If he does nothing more, he will live in history as a great military commander.

From *Battles of Trenton and Princeton*, William S. Stryker, 1898.

— 19 —

My Brave Fellows,
Your Country Is at Stake

A Christmas victory, yes, but what would come next? On January first the enlistment terms of many troops would end. The soldiers lacked shoes and warm clothing. They marched on bleeding feet. Even the horses hauling the cannon had no shoes, and slipped and slid all over the snow and ice. Word came that one of Britain's best generals, Lord Cornwallis, was marching toward the Americans. With the danger of attack so near, Washington saw his army dwindle away. A noncommissioned officer, known to us only as "Sergeant R———," tells what the General did in this crisis:

WHILE WE WERE AT TRENTON, on the last of December, 1776, the time for which I and most of my regiment had enlisted expired. At this trying time General Washington, having now but a little handful of men, and many of them new recruits in which he could place little confidence, ordered our regiment to be paraded, and personally addressed us, urging that we should stay a month longer. He alluded to our recent victory at Trenton, told us that our services were greatly needed, and that we could now do more for our country than we ever could at any future period, and in the most affectionate manner entreated us to stay. The drums beat for volunteers, but not a man turned out. The soldiers, worn down by fatigue and privations, had their hearts fixed on home and the comforts of the domestic circle, and it was hard to forgo the anticipated pleasures of the society of our dearest friends.

The General wheeled his horse about, rode in front of the regiment, and addressing us again said, "My brave fellows, you have done all I asked you to do, and more than could reasonably be expected; but your country is at stake, your wives, your houses, and all that you hold dear. You have worn yourselves out with fatigues and hardships, but we know not how to spare you. If you will consent to stay only one month longer, you will render that service to the cause of liberty, and to your country, which you probably never can do under any other circumstances. The present is emphatically the crisis, which is to decide our destiny."

The drums beat a second time. The soldiers felt the force of the appeal. One said to another, "I will remain if you will." Others remarked, "We cannot go home under such circumstances." A few stepped forth, and their example was immediately followed by nearly all who were fit for duty in the regiment, amounting to about two hundred volunteers. An officer inquired of the General if these men should be enrolled. He replied, "No! men who will volunteer in such a case as this need no enrollment to keep them to their duty."

From "The Battle of Princeton," Sergeant R———, *Pennsylvania Magazine of History and Biography*, XX, 1898.

General George Washington.

111

⟶ 20 ⟵

We Cannot Kill Our Fellowmen

During the time of the revolution many religious groups in America were opposed to taking part in the war. The Quakers, perhaps the best known, were only one among the peace sects who resisted military duty from the earliest days of the colonies. They were persecuted for their pacifist beliefs, but some of the colonies made room for freedom of conscience. When the revolution came, there was no national policy on conscientious objection. Colonial laws often required those who would not serve to do other things: hire a substitute, pay a fine, take such alternative service as work on fortifications, or give up property. Without taking a principled position, a great many other people wanted no part of the war, but simply be let alone to carry on their everyday life.

The peace sects—Quakers, Mennonites, Dunkards, Shakers, and others—took a neutral position during the Revolutionary War. One such sect was the Schwenkfelders, followers of Caspar Schwenkfelder, a sixteenth-century German reformer. They migrated to Pennsylvania from Germany in 1734. On May 1, 1777, the Society issued this declaration on military service:

112

WE WHO ARE KNOWN by the name Schwenkfelders here-by confess and declare that for conscience's sake it is impossible for us to take up arms and kill our fellowmen; we also believe that so far as knowledge of us goes this fact is well known concerning us.

We have hitherto been allowed by our lawmakers to enjoy this liberty of conscience.

We have felt assured of the same freedom of conscience for the future by virtue of the public resolution of Congress and our assembly.

We will with our fellow citizens gladly and willingly bear our due share of the common civil taxes and bur-

The Moravians, nonconformist Christians, were among the Protestant sects committed to the pursuit of peace. This view, made in 1757, shows Bethlehem, Pennsylvania, their main settlement in colonial America.

dens excepting the bearing of arms and weapons.

We cannot in consequence of this take part in the existing militia arrangements, though we would not withdraw ourselves from any other demands of the government.

Whereas, at present, through contempt of the manifested divine goodness and through other sins, heavy burdens, extensive disturbances by war, and diverse military regulations are brought forth and continued;

Whereas, we on the first of this month made a candid declaration concerning present military arrangements to the effect that we cannot on account of conscience take part in said military affairs; and

Whereas, it seems indeed probable that military service will be exacted from many of our people and that on refusal to render such service heavy fines will be imposed;

Therefore, the undersigned who adhere to the apostolic doctrines of the sainted Casper Schwenkfeld and who seek to maintain the same by public services and by instruction of the young have mutually agreed, and herewith united themselves to this end that they will mutually with each other bear such fines as may be imposed on account of refusal for conscience's sake to render military service in case deadly weapons are carried and used. Those on whom such burdens may fall will render a strict account to the managers of the Charity Fund in order that steps may be taken to a proper adjustment.

From *The Schwenkfelders in Pennsylvania, a Historical Sketch*, Pennsylvania German Society Publications, Vol. XIII, Part XII, 1904.

21
Turning Point

In 1777 the British war office came up with a three-pronged plan they were sure would crush the Americans. They would split the colonies by gaining control of New York. First, General John Burgoyne would march from Canada to Albany; second, Colonel Barry St. Leger would advance down the Mohawk River to join him there; and third, Lord William Howe would march north from New York City to meet Burgoyne coming south.

Burgoyne captured Fort Ticonderoga easily, but nothing else went right. St. Leger's force was defeated at Fort Stanwix, north of Albany, and the German mercenary troops hired by the British were beaten at Bennington. Howe chose to attack Philadelphia instead of joining Burgoyne. And Burgoyne himself, in the main battle with the Americans, lost heavily at Saratoga and on October seventeenth was forced to surrender his entire army of about five thousand.

It was a glorious victory for the Americans and a disaster for the British. Saratoga convinced the European enemies of Britain that this was the time to settle old scores. A few months later France signed a treaty with the United States promising to assist her in the fight. Spain, anxious to get back Gibraltar and Minorca, lost to the British in earlier wars, also sent money and supplies to the Americans.

Burgoyne's defeated army was marched to Boston, intending to embark for England. (Instead, however, his men were put in prison camps in Pennsylvania and Virginia.) In a letter to a friend, Hannah Winthrop of Boston caught the note of jubilation as she and other townfolk watched the redcoats straggling into Boston:

LAST THURSDAY, which was a very stormy day, a large number of British troops came softly through the town via Watertown to Prospect Hill. On Friday we heard the Hessians were to make a procession in the same route; we thought we would have nothing to do with them, but view them as they passed.

To be sure, the sight was truly astonishing. I never had the least idea that the Creation produced such a sordid set of creatures in human figure—poor, dirty, emaciated men, great numbers of women who seemed to be the beasts of burden, having a bushel basket on their back, by which they were bent double, the contents seemed to be pots and kettles, various sorts of furniture, children peeping through gridirons and other utensils, some very young infants who were born on the road, the women barefoot, clothed in dirty rags. Such effluvia filled the air while they were passing, had not they been smoking all the time I should have been apprehensive of being contaminated by them.

After a noble-looking advanced guard, General Johnny Burgoyne headed this terrible group on horseback. The other generals also, clothed in blue cloaks. Hessians,

"Gentleman Johnny" Burgoyne, a wealthy Englishman, was a playwright as well as a general. He surrendered his army to the Americans at Saratoga in October 1777, marking a big turning point in the war. This oil portrait is by the distinguished British painter Sir Joshua Reynolds.

Anspachers, Brunswickers, etc., etc., followed on. The Hessian generals gave us a polite bow as they passed. Not so the British, their baggage wagons drawn by poor, half-starved horses. But to bring up the rear, another fine, noble-looking guard of American brawny victorious yeomanry, who assisted in bringing these sons of slavery to terms. Some of our wagons drawn by fat oxen, driven by joyous-looking Yankees, closed the cavalcade.

From *Warren-Adams Letters, 1743–1814*, 1925.

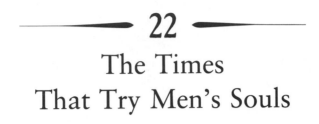

22

The Times
That Try Men's Souls

When news came of the victory at Saratoga, General Washington, with his main army near Philadelphia, was preparing for the winter. Blankets, shoes, clothing, food, were all in terribly short supply. For winter quarters he chose Valley Forge, a crossroads, really, with the ruins of a forge nearby. On a cold gray hillside on December 18, 1777, his tired and hungry men pitched their tents and began to cut down trees to make log cabins. A twenty-seven-year-old Connecticut surgeon in the ranks, Albigence Waldo, noted conditions in his diary:

DECEMBER 21.   Preparations made for huts. Provisions scarce. . . . Sent a letter to my wife. Heartily wish myself at home. My skin and eyes are almost spoiled with continual smoke. A general cry through the camp this evening among the soldiers, "No meat! No meat!" The distant vales echoed back the melancholy sound, "No meat! No meat!"

"What have you for your dinners, boys?"

"Nothing but fire cake and water, sir."

At night, "Gentlemen, the supper is ready."

"What is your supper, lads?"

"Fire cake and water, sir."

Very poor beef has been drawn in our camp the greater part of this season. A butcher, bringing a quarter of this kind of beef into camp one day, had white buttons on the knees of his breeches. A soldier cries out, "There, there, Tom, is some more of your fat beef. By my soul, I can see the butcher's breeches buttons through it."

DECEMBER 2.   Lay excessive cold and uncomfortable last night. My eyes are started out from their orbits like a rabbit's eyes, occasioned by a great cold and smoke.

"What have you got for breakfast, lads?"

"Fire cake and water, sir."

The Lord send that our Commissary of Purchases may live on fire cake and water till their glutted guts are turned to pasteboard.

DECEMBER 25, CHRISTMAS.   We are still in tents when we ought to be in huts. The poor sick suffer much in tents this cold weather. But we now treat them differently from what they used to be at home under the inspection of old women and Dr. Bolus Linctus. We give them mutton and grog and a capital medicine once in a

In "the winter of despair," 1777–78, about 11,000 of Washington's men were encamped at Valley Forge. A great many were barefoot, hungry, and sick, and 3,000 died. Yet nearby the civilians enjoyed good food and warm clothing.

while to start the disease from its foundation at once. We avoid Piddling Pills, Powders, Bolus's Linctus's Cordials, and all such insignificant matters whose powers are only rendered important by causing the patient to vomit up his money instead of his disease. But very few of the sick men die.

From "Valley Forge, 1777–1778, Diary," Albigence Waldo,
Pennsylvania Magazine of History, XXI, 1897.

Winter in those times was no season for fighting. But now and then there was a bit of action. John McCasland, a two-month volunteer in the Pennsylvania militia, served at Valley Forge as a scout. Later he recalled this event:

WE HAD NO FIGHTING, but we had to scour the country to prevent the Hessians from plundering and destroying property, who generally [went] out in small gangs. And at different times we took Hessians prisoners and delivered them to General Washington at Valley Forge.

And on one occasion, sixteen of us were ranging about hunting Hessians, and we suspected Hessians to be at a large and handsome mansion house in Bucks County, Pennsylvania, about sixteen miles from Philadelphia. We approached near the house and discovered a large Hessian standing in the yard with his gun, as a sentinel we supposed, and by a unanimous vote of the company present it was agreed on that Major McCorman or myself, who were good marksmen, should shoot him (McCorman was then a private). We cast lots, and it fell to my lot to shoot the Hessian. I did not like to shoot a man down in cold blood. The company present knew I was a good marksman, and I concluded to break his thigh. I shot with a rifle and aimed at his hip. He had a large iron tobacco box in his breeches pocket, and I hit the box, the ball glanced, and it entered his thigh and scaled the bone of the thigh on the outside. He fell and then rose. We scaled the yard fence and surrounded the house. They saw their situation and were evidently disposed to surrender. They could not speak English, and we could not understand their language. At length one of the Hessians came out of the cellar with a large bottle of rum and advanced with it at arm's length as a flag of truce. The family had abandoned the house, and the Hessians had possession. They were twelve in number. We took them prisoners and carried them to Valley Forge and delivered them up to General Washington.

From "Deposition of John McCasland, 1832." Revolutionary War pension application, National Archive.

Valley Forge became a symbol of American courage in the face of great trials. But much of the suffering could have been avoided if Congress and the civilians had only carried out their obligations. Their failure to produce supplies persisted through the war. A winter later, 1778–79, encamped at Morristown, New Jersey, Ebenezer Huntington, who had left Yale to join the army and now was a lieutenant colonel, could still bitterly complain. He had heard the French were bringing help, but in a letter to his brother he urged the people of Connecticut to send aid to the army:

THE RASCALLY STUPIDITY which now prevails in the country at large is beyond all descriptions. They patiently see our illustrious commander at the head of twenty-five hundred or three thousand ragged, though virtuous and good, men and be obliged to put up with what no troops ever did before.

Why don't you reinforce your army, feed them, clothe, and pay them? Why do you suffer the enemy to have a foothold on the continent? You can prevent it. Send your men to the field, believe you are Americans, not suffer yourselves to be duped into the thought that the French will relieve you and fight your battles. It is your own superiorness that induced Congress to ask foreign aid.

122

It is a reflection too much for a soldier. You don't deserve to be free men, unless you can believe it yourselves. When they arrive, they will not put up with such treatment as your army have done. They will not serve week after week without meat, without clothing, and paid in filthy rags.

I despise my countrymen. I wish I could say I was not born in America. I once gloried in it, but am now ashamed of it. If you do your duty, though late, you may finish the war this campaign. You must immediately fill your regiments and pay your troops in hard monies. They cannot exist as soldiers otherwise. The insults and neglects which the army have met with from the country beggars all description. It must go no farther; they can endure it no longer. I have wrote in a passion. Indeed, I am scarce ever free from it . . . and all this for my cowardly countrymen who flinch at the very time when their exertions are wanted and hold their purse strings as though they would damn the world rather than part with a dollar to their army.

From *Letters Written During the American Revolution*,
Ebenezer Huntington, 1915.

— 23 —

Death Ceased to Terrify

The hardships soldiers went through were sometimes beyond bearing. At Morristown it was reported men roasted their old shoes and ate them, and some devoured their pet dogs. Starvation brought men to fight one another for a morsel of food, to steal from fellow soldiers or the local people, and to desert. Although Washington felt for them, and did his best to meet their needs, he would not tolerate breach of discipline. Courts-martial sentenced deserters to be shot or hung, and condemned others to the dungeon on bread and water, to run the gauntlet, or to take one hundred lashes on the bare back. Dr. James Thacher, a young surgeon's mate from Cape Cod, witnessed many such punishments:

THE CULPRIT BEING SECURELY TIED to a tree or post receives on his naked back the number of lashes assigned him, by a whip formed of several small knotted cords, which sometimes cut through the skin at every stroke. However strange it may appear, a soldier will often receive the severest stripes without uttering a groan or once shrieking from the lash, even while the blood flows freely from his lacerated wounds. This must be ascribed to stubbornness or pride. They have, however, adopted a method which they say mitigates the anguish in some measure. It is by putting between the teeth a leaden bullet, on which they chew while under the lash, till it is made quite flat and jagged. In some instances of incorrigible villains, it is adjudged by the court that the culprit receive his punishment at several different times, a certain number of stripes repeated at intervals of two or three days, in which case the wounds are in a state of inflammation and the skin rendered more sensibly tender, and the terror of the punishment is greatly aggravated.

From A Military Journal During the American Revolutionary War,
James Thacher, 2nd ed., 1827.

Capture by the enemy was sure in that war to be a terrible trial. Neither side was able to take humane care of its prisoners. Nor did they develop a system for the orderly exchange of captives or their release. No reliable figures exist on how many prisoners were taken, but the guess is it was about the same number on both sides. Without planning, both sides used whatever was at hand to house prisoners. It might be a jail, a barracks, a barroom, a church, a mine, a ship, a warehouse. No matter which, captured soldiers could be sure it would be miserable and often savage.

James Morris, a lieutenant in a Connecticut regiment, was captured by the British at the battle of Germantown in October 1777. He recalls the cold and starvation he suffered with the others penned up in Philadelphia:

I ARRIVED AT THE JAIL in Philadelphia about eight o'clock in the evening. I was locked into a cold room destitute of everything but cold stone walls and bare floors—no kind of a seat to sit on—all total darkness, no water to drink or a morsel to eat; destitute a blanket to cover me, I groped about my solitary cell, and in moving about I found that there were two or three persons lying on the floor asleep. I said nothing to them, nor they to me. I stood on my feet and leaned my back against the wall, and sometimes moved about the room, and then to change my position I sat on the floor, but no sleep nor slumber; parched with thirst and no one on which I could call for a drop of water. In short, it was a long, dismal, dreary and most gloomy night that I ever beheld.

I reflected on the miseries of the damned in that eternal, friendless prison of despair, but still hope hovered around my soul that I should see another morning. Morning finally arrived, and at a late hour, we were furnished with some very hard sea bread and salted pork, and I was able to obtain some water to drink. Being altogether moneyless I could purchase nothing for my comfort. I pretty soon sold my watch for half its value, and with the money I received for it I was able to procure some food pleasant to my taste. I wholly gave up my allowance of provisions to the poor soldiers.

At this time and in this jail were confined 700 prisoners of war. A few small rooms were sequestered for the officers. Each room must contain sixteen men, we fully covered the whole floor when we lay down to

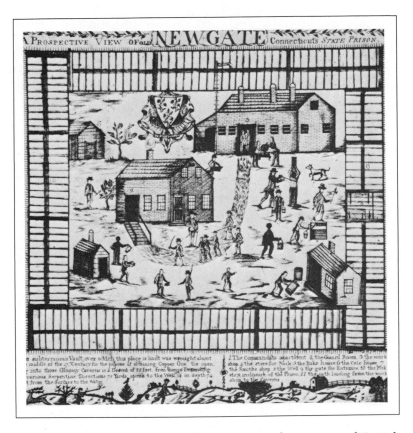

The prison yard at Newgate, Connecticut, where captured British soldiers were confined. It was built above an abandoned copper mine.

sleep, and the poor soldiers were shut into rooms of the same magnitude with double the number. The poor soldiers were soon seized with the jailfever, as it was called, and it swept off in the course of three months 400 men, who were all buried in one continued grave without coffins. The length of a man was the width of the grave, lying three deep one upon another. I thus lived in jail from the 5th of October 1777, till the month of May 1778. Our number daily decreasing by the King of Terrors. Such a scene of mortality I never witnessed before. Death was so frequent that it ceased to terrify. It ceased to warn; it ceased to alarm survivors.

From "James Morris Memoirs," Town Clerk's Office, Morris, Connecticut.

Rather than suffer these conditions, many chose escape. One of the most dramatic flights from captivity was engineered by Lieutenant Charles Bulkeley of the United States Navy. In March 1778 he was captured off Barbados while serving on the Alfred. *His journal records his imprisonment and escape:*

WE SAILED FOR ENGLAND and arrived at Portsmouth, were landed at Gosport and examined and confined in Fortune Prison about one mile from Gosport. We were confined in the upper part of the prison, with the liberty of the yard in the daytime, and at night lamps were placed all around the prison to prevent escapes. In consequence of complaints received, a Presbyterian priest by the name of Wren was permitted to come into the prison weekly and to supply many of the wants that the prisoners stood in need of. We now made arrangements to make our escape—we cut through the floor into the Black Hole and then through another floor for the purpose of digging out, the Black Hole being the place that the prisoners were confined in on account of any offences they may have committed.

128

Before breaking out we agreed in case we got separated to meet at a certain place in London. We dug in a slanting direction so that there might be dirt overhead sufficient that it might not cave in. The tools we had to work with were an old chisel and a broken fencing foil. We made small bags to put the dirt in; we found great difficulty in secreting the dirt at first; we put some in our chest. The fireplace below being stopped up, we took some bricks out of the chimney in the upper loft and took the bags and lowered them down to the bottom and with a tripping line emptied them so that there might not be any noise heard from the falling of the dirt.

We were over three weeks in digging out. We made a lottery for the purpose of having regular turns in going out, for the prevention of confusion and noise, the guard being very near to the hole dug for our escape. Before going out we put a pair of trousers, shirt and stocking, over our other clothes and covered our heads and hats, and after getting out we took them off and threw them away. The hole was so small that Captain Harrison of Virginia, after trying to get out was wedged in; we were obliged to pull him back by the legs.

After our escape we went to Gosport for the purpose of crossing to Portsmouth. Three of us got a post chaise (Mr. Richards having separated from us by accident). We had to go by the prison just at daylight and before any alarm was given, and arrived at London in the afternoon, being 75 miles, and here we all again met and stayed a few days and visited St. Paul's church and the Tower and were well worth seeing. Captain Welch and Lieutenant Hamilton went to Holland and Lieutenant

Richards and myself went to Deal, 75 miles from London, and got a passage in an open smuggler's boat and crossed the channel for France in the night and landed at Calais.

From "Charles Bulkeley Journal," New London Historical Society, Shaw Mansion, New London, Connecticut.

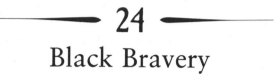

24

Black Bravery

Only weeks after the first guns of the revolution fired at Lexington and Concord, the Massachusetts legislature decided it was "inconsistent with the principles" for which Americans were fighting to let slaves join the army. But if slaveholders should free black men first, and then they volunteered for service, they would be welcomed. Blacks who had never been slaves did fight from the first in the American ranks. Salem Poor and several other Blacks fought at Breed's Hill—Poor so gallantly that fourteen officers sent a petition to the legislature declaring that he "behaved like an experienced officer, as well as an excellent soldier," and added that "a reward was due to so great and distinguished a character."

But the bravery of black soldiers did not make America enlist more of them. Southern delegates to the Con-

130

tinental Congress opposed it. Their states feared that if many Blacks enlisted, the slaves would become restless and might even revolt. The northern delegates, anxious for unity at any cost, joined with the southerners in ordering General Washington to stop recruiting Blacks. The Blacks already in service were angry, but unable to change the decision. Many whites in the north pointed out that if America did not let Blacks fight, the British would promise them freedom in return for joining their side. Which is just what happened. Hundreds of slaves fled the plantations to join the British forces. It frightened the slaveowners; they decided to let some Blacks join the army.

As the American plight grew desperate, Washington decided to ignore Congress and permit Blacks to enlist. Congress then hastily approved his decision and the states began to offer slaves freedom in return for service under arms. Rhode Island, for example, on February 14, 1778, passed this slave enlistment bill, initiated by army officers:

WHEREAS for the preservation of the rights and liberties of the United States, it is necessary that the whole powers of government should be exerted in recruiting the Continental battalions; and whereas, His Excellency General Washington hath enclosed to this state a proposal made to him by Brigadier General Varnum, to enlist into the two battalions, raising by this state, such slaves as should be willing to enter into the service; and whereas, history affords us frequent precedents of the wisest, the freest, and bravest nations having liberated their slaves, and enlisted them as soldiers to fight in defense of their country; and also whereas, the enemy, with a great force, have taken possession of the capital, and of a greater part of this state; and this state is obliged to raise a very considerable number of troops for its own immediate defense, whereby it is in a manner rendered impossible for this state to furnish recruits for the said two battalions, without adopting the said measure so recommended.

It is voted and resolved, that every able-bodied Negro, mulatto, or Indian man slave in this state, may enlist into either of the said two battalions, to serve during the continuance of the present war with Great Britain.

That every slave, so enlisting, shall be entitled to, and receive all the bounties, wages, and encouragements, allowed by the Continental Congress, to any soldier enlisting into their service.

It is further voted and resolved, that every slave, so enlisting shall, upon his passing muster before Colonel Christopher Greene, be immediately discharged from the service of his master or mistress, and be absolutely FREE, as though he had never been encumbered with any kind of servitude or slavery.

And in case such slave shall, by sickness or otherwise, be rendered unable to maintain himself, he shall not be chargeable to his master or his mistress; but shall be supported at the expense of the state.

And whereas, slaves have been, by the laws, deemed the property of their owners, and therefore compensa-

Peter Salem could well have been the black man at the extreme right, holding a rifle. He fought in the Battle of Bunker Hill. A Massachusetts slave, he was given his freedom so he could enlist. Earlier he was at Lexington and Concord. John Turnbull painted the Bunker Hill fight although he was not present. He may have meant the black soldier to be symbolic of the many serving in the Revolutionary army.

tion ought to be made to the owners for the loss of their service;

It is further voted and resolved, that there be allowed, and paid by this state, to the owner, for every such slave so enlisting a sum according to his worth; at a price not exceeding £120 for the most valuable slave; and in proportion for a slave of less value.

From *Records of the State of Rhode Island and Providence Plantations in New England*, John R. Bartlett, ed., 1856–65.

25

War in Indian Country

The Indians living in the forest along the immense frontier were a constant concern all through the revolution. Most of them sided with the British, as they had ever since the British ousted the French from North America in 1763. Skilled at playing off one group of whites against another, they went with the winners. Some Indians remained friendly to the Americans, and others tried to remain neutral. Most, however, saw the war as a chance to halt the Americans' pushing relentlessly into their hunting grounds. The British armed, supplied, and organized the Indians, but they did it badly.

Still, the border warfare did great damage to the Americans. Fighting flared up year after year on several frontiers. The Americans had few Indian allies against the number who fought alongside the British. That the British would unleash Indian terror infuriated the Americans, who only regretted they could not match it.

During Burgoyne's frustrated attempt in 1777 to cut off New York State by an invasion, his Indian allies raided the countryside, terrifying the civilians. What they did was reported in a letter from William Weeks, paymaster of a New Hampshire regiment:

THERE IS A VERY GOOD CROP in these parts, but soon comes a desolation; wherever we march we keep our

A scene in the grim border warfare, where most of the Indians fought as allies of the British.

horses in the fields among corn and oats, so that the enemy, if they gain the ground, may have poor fare for them and their horses. Tories are very troublesome here—many of them take up arms against us and lurk in the woods with the Indians waiting for a scalp. It is believed the Tories have scalped many of their countrymen, as there is a premium from Burgoyne for scalps. They are daily taken and brought in by our scouts and I believe some of them will swing very soon.

The Indians treat both sexes with the same barbarity, have killed and scalped whole families together—men, women, and children. At one place, as our men were passing, they saw a man, his wife and children scalped (by those savages), gaping and expiring and the hogs rooting their bodies.

A few days ago I rode a little distance from camp where we had a few men stationed to guard the sick. I had just passed the place where a party of Indians happened to lay and stopped at the first house talking with an officer. As I sat upon my horse, out rushed those Indians and fired at some men swimming in the water and chased some as they were passing. I, seeing this, screamed to the guard to pursue them, and rode toward them. They discharged their pieces toward us, and fired one ball into the house not far from the door where I was. Immediately upon our pursuing them they ran into the woods and got off. We were in such haste they had not time to get a scalp. They killed two; one shot in the water, who got out and ran a considerable distance before he fell. Since then they have cut off more of our men—one hundred Indians in the woods do no more harm than 1,000 British troops. They have been the death of many brave fellows—I hope they will meet with their reward for their cursed cruelty.

From *Five Straws Gathered from Revolutionary Fields*,
Hiram Bingham, 1901.

To the west, on the frontier beyond the Appalachians, the Indians were used by the British to keep the Americans off balance. To end their attacks, Virginia in 1778 dispatched Lieutenant Colonel George Rogers Clark with about two hundred frontiersmen. A giant of a redhead, in his mid-twenties, Clark opposed the Indian and Tory

136

forces of English Colonel Henry Hamilton. Near Vincennes, a frontier settlement occupied by Hamilton, Clark's men attacked a party of Indians returning from a scouting expedition. The Americans killed two Indians and wounded one. What Clark's men then did to their captives was recorded by Hamilton from reports he received:

THE REST WERE SURROUNDED and taken bound to the village where, being set in the street opposite the fort gate, they were put to death, notwithstanding a truce at that moment existed. . . . One of them was tomahawked immediately. The rest, sitting on the ground in a ring, bound, seeing by the fate of their comrade what they had to expect, the next on his left sung his death song and was in turn tomahawked. The rest underwent the same. . . . One only was saved by the intercession of a rebel officer who pleaded for him, telling Colonel Clark that the savage's father had formerly saved his life.

The chief of this party, after having the hatchet stuck in his head, took it out himself and delivered it to the inhuman monster who struck him first, who repeated his stroke a second and a third time, after which the miserable spectacle was dragged by the rope around his neck to the river, thrown in, and suffered to spend still a few moments of life in fruitless strugglings. . . .

Colonel Clark, yet reeking with the blood of these unhappy victims, came to the esplanade before the fort gate, where I had agreed to meet him and treat of the surrender of the garrison. He spoke with rapture of his

137

late achievement, while he washed the blood from his
hand stained in this inhuman sacrifice.

From "Report," Henry Hamilton, Great Britain Mss. Comission,
Manuscripts of Mrs. Stopford-Sackville, Vol. II.

*Hamilton's report was not an invented atrocity story.
Clark freely admitted it; he did it to convince the Indians
that the British couldn't protect them as promised. Hamilton himself was believed guilty of offering rewards to
Indians not for prisoners but for scalps, thus encour-
aging them to kill their captives.*

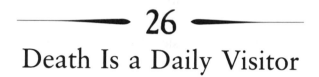

26

Death Is a Daily Visitor

*Disease killed far more men than bullets, swords, or
bayonets in the Revolutionary War—it destroyed ten
times as many, was one observer's estimate. Soldiers felt
less danger on the battlefield than in the hospital. Medicine was still medieval, far from the modern practise
we know today. No one understood infection, surgery
was butchery, and anesthetics were unknown.*

*In America there was but a handful of skilled doctors,
effective drugs were almost two centuries in the future,
there were few hospitals, and medicines, instruments, ban-*

dages, and bedding were almost always lacking just when needed most.

Plans to meet the constant medical emergencies were missing, and so were the funds. Pay for military physicians and aides was miserable. Wounded or sick soldiers had to survive or die almost on their own. A glimpse of the medical side of the military is given in the journal of Dr. Lewis Beebe of Massachusetts, who served in the Canadian campaign of 1776:

FRIDAY, JUNE 7.   Last evening one died of the smallpox, and early this morning one of the colic; at 10 A.M. one of the nervous fever. Here in the hospital is to be seen at the same time some dead, some dying, others at the point of death, some whistling, some singing, and many cursing and swearing. This is a strange composition and its chief intention has not as yet been discovered; however it appears very plain that it is wonderfully calculated for a campaign, and, if applied properly and in time, is very efficacious to prevent anything that is serious or concerning futurity. Visited many of the sick in the hospital—was moved with a compassionate feeling for poor distressed soldiers, [who] when they are taken sick, are thrown into this dirty, stinking place and left to take care of themselves. No attendance, no provision made, but what must be loathed and abhorred by all both well and sick.

MONDAY, JUNE 10.   This day died two in Colonel Patterson's regiment with the smallpox. No intelligence of importance comes to hand this day, except orders, from the great Mr. Brigadier General Arnold, for Colonel Poor with his regiment to proceed to Sorrell immediately. Is not this a politic plan, especially since there is not ten men in the regiment but what has either now got the smallpox or taken the infection? Some men love to command, however ridiculous their orders may appear. But I am apt to think we shall remain in this garrison for the present. It is enough to confuse and distract a rational man to be surgeon to a regiment. Nothing to be heard from morning to night but "Doctor! Doctor! Doctor!" from every side till one is deaf, dumb, and blind, and almost dead; add to all this, we have nothing to eat; thus poor soldiers live sometimes better, but never worse. . . .

This morning had Colonel Poor's orders to repair to Isle aux Naux to take care of the sick there; accordingly sailed in a batteau, and arrived there about 3 P.M. Was struck with amazement upon my arrival to see the vast crowds of poor distressed creatures. Language cannot describe nor imagination paint the scenes of misery and distress the soldiery endure. Scarcely a tent upon this isle but what contains one or more in distress and continually groaning and calling for relief—but in vain! Requests of this nature are as little regarded as the singing of crickets in a summer's evening. The most shocking of all spectacles was to see a large barn crowded full of men with this disorder, many of which could not see, speak or walk. One—nay, two—had large maggots, an inch long, crawl out of their ears; [they] were on almost every part of the body. No mortal will ever believe what these suffered unless they were eyewitnesses. Fuller appeared to be near his end. General Sullivan set fire to all the armed vessels, 3 gundalows and fort at Chambly, and at evening came all his army, with all the stores and baggage, to St. Johns.

WEDNESDAY, JUNE 26.   The regiment is in a most deplorable situation; between 4 and 500 now in the height of the smallpox. Death is now become a daily visitant in the camps, but as little regarded as the singing of birds.

From "Journal," Lewis Beebe, *Pennsylvania Magazine of History and Biography*, LIX.

27

I'm Not Afraid
of the Cannonballs

Women of this era found their lives changed by the time the revolution ended. Abigail Adams had much experience running John's business affairs while he was off politicking. Women living on the frontier had always known danger, but the guerrilla fighting they witnessed made war a reality. The women whose husbands went off to fight learned much about the world beyond the family hearth as they took on new and challenging roles. Women began to act collectively, supporting the cause of liberty together, raising money, gathering or making supplies, boycotting British goods, resisting profiteering.

But many women did not stay at home. Married soldiers often took their families with them. In the military camps there were sometimes as many women and children as there were soldiers. Of course, when a battle was to be fought, the men separated from their families. But not always. For some women traveled with the army to serve as cooks, laundresses, seamstresses, bakers. Few seem to have left any record of their doings. One who did was Sarah Osborn. Born in Blooming Grove, New York, she was to marry a blacksmith who enlisted as a commissary sergeant in a New York regiment. At his insistence Sarah "volunteered" to work alongside Aaron Osborn for the duration. (It would be three years for her.) In 1837, she put in for a war widow's pension, and got it. The following passages are from her statement given to a court clerk when she applied for the pension. "Deponent" refers to Sarah. She was marching with the troops toward Philadelphia, prior to the siege of Yorktown, when we pick up her story:

THEY CONTINUED THEIR MARCH to Philadelphia, deponent on horseback through the streets, and arrived at a place toward the Schuylkill where the British had burnt some houses, where they encamped for the afternoon and night. Being out of bread, deponent was employed in baking the afternon and evening. Deponent recollects no females but Sergeant Lamberson's and Lieutenant Forman's wives and a colored woman by the name of Letta. The Quaker ladies who came round urged deponent to stay, but her husband said, "No, he could not leave her behind." Accordingly, next day they continued their march from day to day till they arrived at Baltimore, where deponent and her said husband and the forces . . . embarked on board a vessel and sailed down the Chesapeake. There were several vessels along, and deponent was in the foremost. . . . They continued sail until they had got up the St. James River as far as the tide would carry them, about twelve miles from the mouth, and then landed, and the tide being spent, they had a fine time catching sea lobsters, which they ate.

They, however, marched immediately for a place called Williamsburg, deponent alternately on horseback and on foot. There arrived, they remained two days till the army all came in by land and then marched for Yorktown. . . . The York troops were posted at the right, the Connecticut troops next, and the French to the left. In about one day or less than a day, they reached the place of encampment about one mile from Yorktown. Deponent was on foot, and the other females above named, and her said husband still on the commissary's guard.

Deponent's attention was arrested by the appearance of a large plain between them and Yorktown and an entrenchment thrown up. She also saw a number of dead Negroes lying round their encampment, whom she

143

understood the British had driven out of the town and left to starve, or were first starved and then thrown out. Deponent took her stand just back of the American tents, say about a mile from the town, and busied herself washing, mending, and cooking for the soldiers, in which she was assisted by the other females; some men washed their own clothing. She heard the roar of the artillery for a number of days, and the last night the Americans

The legendary heroine of the Battle of Monmouth was known as Molly Pitcher. Born Mary Ludwig, she worked as a domestic servant and married the barber John Hays, who enlisted as a gunner in the artillery. She joined her husband in camp, washing and cooking for the soldiers and nursing them. During the Monmouth fight she carried water in a pitcher to the parched soldiers. When her husband fell wounded, she took his place and kept loading his cannon till victory was won. This is one depiction of her bravery.

threw up entrenchments; it was a misty, foggy night, rather wet but not rainy. Every soldier threw up for himself, as she understood, and she afterward saw and went into the entrenchments. Deponent's said husband was there throwing up entrenchments, and deponent cooked and carried in beef, and bread, and coffee (in a gallon pot) to the soldiers in the entrenchment.

On one occasion when deponent was thus employed carrying in provisions, she met General Washington, who asked her if she "was not afraid of the cannon-balls"?

She replied, "No, the bullets would not cheat the gallows," that "It would not do for the men to fight and starve, too."

They dug entrenchments nearer and nearer to York-town every night or two till the last. While digging that, the enemy fired very heavy till about nine o'clock next morning, then stopped, and the drums from the enemy beat excessively. . . .

The drums continued beating, and all at once the officers hurrahed and swung their hats, and deponent asked them, "What is the matter now?"

One of them replied, "Are not you soldier enough to know what it means?"

Deponent replied, "No."

They then replied, "The British have surrendered."

Deponent, having provisions ready, carried the same down to the entrenchments that morning, and four of the soldiers whom she was in the habit of cooking for ate their breakfasts.

Deponent stood on one side of the road and the American officers upon the other side when the British officers came out of the town and rode up to the American officers and delivered up their swords, which the deponent thinks were returned again, and the British officers rode right on before the army, who marched out beating and playing a melancholy tune, their drums covered with black handkerchiefs and their fifes with black ribbons tied around them, into an old field and there grounded their arms and then returned into town again to await their destiny. Deponent recollects seeing a great many American officers, some on horseback and some on foot, but cannot call them all by name. Washington, Lafayette, and Clinton were among the number. The British general at the head of the army was a large, portly man, full face, and the tears rolled down his cheeks as he passed along. She does not recollect his name, but it was not Cornwallis. She saw the latter afterward and noticed his being a man of diminutive appearance and having cross eyes.

On going into town, she noticed two dead Negroes lying by the market house. She had the curiosity to go into a large building that stood nearby, and there she noticed the cupboards smashed to pieces and china dishes and other ware strewed around upon the floor, and among the rest a pewter cover to a hot basin that had a handle on it. She picked it up, supposing it to belong to the British, but the governor came in and claimed it as his, but said he would have the name of giving it away as it was the last one out of twelve that he could see, and accordingly presented it to deponent, and she afterward brought it home with her to Orange County and sold it for old pewter, which she has a hundred times regretted.

From Military Pension Records, National Archives.

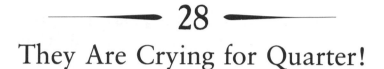

28

They Are Crying for Quarter!

Late in 1778 the British turned their attention to the south. They believed its Loyalists were numerous and eager to help. British troops took Savannah, but did not make a major effort until the spring of 1780, when they captured Charleston, along with five thousand prisoners. Then came news from the north of the arrival of a French fleet and army. Sir Henry Clinton, the British commander, returned to New York, leaving Lord Cornwallis to head his southern forces.

While Washington stood watch over Clinton in New York, he sent what troops he could spare to the south. The British beat the Americans at Camden, in South Carolina, and again at Guilford Court House, in North Carolina. The southern states seemed lost, and Cornwallis felt confident of an early victory. But then a fresh resistance rose up. American backwoodsmen formed into guerrilla bands and wiped out twelve hundred Loyalists at King's Mountain on the border between the Carolinas in October 1780. It was a crushing defeat that terrified the British and the Loyalists while it rekindled the fervor of the patriots.

James Collins, a sixteen-year-old soldier, was with the American riflemen as they headed for King's Mountain to attack the Loyalists squatting at the top:

EVERYONE ATE what he could get, and slept in his own blanket, sometimes eating raw turnips and often resorting to a little parched corn, which, by the by, I have often thought, if a man would eat a mess of parched corn and swallow two or three spoonfuls of honey, then take a good draught of cold water, he could pass longer without suffering than with any other diet he could use. On Saturday morning, October 7, 1780, the sky was overcast with clouds, and at times a light mist of rain falling. . . .

We were soon in motion, every man throwing four or five balls in his mouth to prevent thirst, also to be in readiness to reload quick. The shot of the enemy soon began to pass over us like hail. The first shock was quickly over, and for my own part, I was soon in a profuse sweat. My lot happened to be in the center where the severest part of the battle was fought. We soon attempted to climb the hill, but were fiercely charged upon and forced to fall back to our first position. We tried a second time, but met the same fate. The fight then seemed to become more furious.

Their leader, Ferguson, came in full view, within rifle

shot, as if to encourage his men, who by this time were falling very fast. He soon disappeared. We took to the hill a third time. The enemy gave way. When we had gotten near the top, some of our leaders roared out, "Hurrah, my brave fellows! Advance! They are crying for quarter!"

From *Autobiography of a Revolutionary Soldier*, James P. Collins, 1859.

On the other side of the mountain was another sixteen-year-old American private, Thomas Young. His shoes lost, he moved barefoot up the slope, lugging his heavy old musket charged with two balls. He tells of the action on his front:

THE ORDERS WERE at the firing of the first gun for every man to raise a whoop, rush forward, and fight his way as he best could. When our division came up to the . . . mountain, we dismounted and Colonel Benjamin Roebuck drew us a little to the left and commenced the attack; I well remember how I behaved.

Ben Hollingsworth and myself took right up the side of the mountain and fought from tree to tree . . . to the summit. I recollect I stood behind one tree and fired until the bark was nearly all knocked off and my eyes pretty well filled with it. One fellow shaved me pretty close, for his bullet took a piece out of my own gun stock. Before I was aware of it, I found myself apparently between my own regiment and the enemy, as I judged from seeing the paper which the Whigs wore in their hats and

149

the pine knots the Tories wore in theirs, these being the badges of distinction.

On the top of the mountain, in the thickest of the fight, I saw Colonel Williams fall. . . . I had seen him but once before that day. It was in the beginning of the action, as he charged by me at full speed around the mountain. Toward the summit, a ball struck his horse under the jaw, when he commenced stamping as if he were in a nest of yellow jackets. Colonel Williams threw his reins over the animal's neck, sprang to the ground, and dashed onward.

The moment I heard the cry that Colonel Williams was shot I ran to his assistance, for I loved him as a father. He had ever been so kind to me and almost always carried a cake in his pocket for me and his little son Joseph. They . . . sprinkled some water in his face. He revived, and his first words were, "For God's sake, boys, don't give up the hill!" . . . I left him in the arms of his son Daniel, and returned to the field to avenge his fate.

From "Memoir," Thomas Young, *The Orion*, Vol. III, October, 1843.

The next morning, Sunday, James Collins awoke to a sad and appalling scene:

THE WIVES and children of the poor Tories came in, in great numbers. Their husbands, fathers, and brothers lay dead in heaps, while others lay wounded or dying. . . . We proceeded to bury the dead, but it was badly done. They were thrown into convenient piles and covered with old logs, the bark of old trees and rocks, yet not so as to secure them from becoming a prey to the beasts of the forest, or the vultures of the air; and the wolves later became so plenty, that it was dangerous for anyone to be out at night for several miles around. Also the hogs in the neighborhood gathered into the place to devour the flesh of men, inasmuch as numbers chose to live on little meat rather than eat their hogs, though they were fat. Half of the dogs in the country were said to be mad and were put to death. I saw myself in passing the place, a few weeks after, all parts of the human frame . . . scattered in every direction. . . .

In the evening, there was a distribution . . . of the plunder, and we were dismissed. My father and myself drew two fine horses, two guns, and some articles of clothing with a share of powder and lead. Every man repaired to his tent or home. It seemed like a calm after a heavy storm . . . and for a short time, every man could visit his home, or his neighbor without being afraid.

From *Autobiography*, Collins, 1859.

— 29 —

It Was a Mutiny

The victory at King's Mountain was good news for Washington, but his joy was abruptly cut short as 1781 opened. Troops in winter quarters at Morristown decided they would no longer submit passively to their grievances: no pay for months, rags for clothing, dry bread and water for food. And most painful of all, the fact that those who had enlisted for "three years or the duration of the war" now found that the duration would be longer than the three years. To make it even worse, on the night of January 1, 1781, recruiting agents came to the neighborhood to offer twenty-five dollars cash for new recruits.

What happened was mutiny by the Pennsylvania troops. Lieutenant Enos Reeves describes it in this letter:

I WENT ON THE PARADE and found numbers in small groups whispering and busily running up and down the line. In a short time a gun was fired upon the right and answered by one on the right of the Second Brigade, and a skyrocket thrown from the center of the first, which was accompanied by a general huzza throughout the line, and the soldiers running out with their arms, accoutrements and knapsacks.

I immediately found it was a mutiny, and that the

guns and skyrocket were the signals. The officers in general exerted themselves to keep the men quiet, and keep them from turning out. We each applied himself to his own company, endeavored to keep them in their huts and lay by their arms, which they would do while we were present, but the moment we left one hut to go to another, they would be out again. Their excuse was they thought it was an alarm and the enemy coming on.

Next they began to move in crowds to the parade . . . which was the place appointed for their rendezvous. Lieutenant White of our regiment, in endeavoring to stop one of those crowds, was shot through the thigh, and Captain Samuel Tolbert, in opposing another party, was shot through the body, of which he is very ill. They continued huzzaing and firing in a riotous manner, so that it soon became dangerous for an officer to oppose them by force. We then left them to go their own way. . . .

About this time General Wayne and several field officers (mounted) arrived. General Wayne and Colonel Butler spoke to them for a considerable time, but it had no effect. Their answer was they had been wronged and were determined to see themselves righted. He replied that he would right them as far as in his power. They rejoined, it was out of his power; their business was not with the officers but with the Congress and the Governor and Council of the State—'twas they had wronged and they must right. With that, several platoons fired over the General's head. The General called out, "If you mean to kill me, shoot me at once—here's my breast!" opening his coat. They replied it was not their intention to hurt or disturb an officer of the line (two or three individuals excepted); that they had nothing against their officers and they would oppose any person that would attempt anything of the kind.

A part of the Fourth Regiment was paraded and led by Captain Campbell to recapture the cannon; they were ordered to charge and rush on. They charged, but would not advance, then dispersed and left the officer alone. Soon after a soldier from the mob made a charge upon Lieutenant Colonel Butler, who was obliged to retreat between the huts to save his life. He went around one

"I damn my country as void of gratitude!" said one of the soldiers encamped at Morristown, New Jersey, in the freezing winter of 1781. How can the Congress let us starve? the men asked. In the print they launch a mutiny as officers try to hold them off.

hut and the soldier around another to meet him, met Captain Bettin who was coming down the alley, who, seeing a man coming toward him on a charge, charged his spontoon to oppose him, when the fellow fired his piece and shot the captain through the body and he died two hours later.

About twelve o'clock they sent parties to relieve or seize the old camp guard, and posted sentinels all around the camp. At one o'clock they moved off toward the left of the line with the cannon, and when they reached the center they fired a shot. As they came down the line, they turned the soldiers out of every hut, and those who would not go with them were obliged to hide till they were gone. They continued huzzaing and a disorderly firing till they went off about two o'clock, with drums and fifes playing, under command of the sergeants, in regular platoons, with a front and rear guard.

General Wayne met them as they were marching off and endeavored to persuade them back, but to no purpose. He then inquired which way they were going, and they replied either to Trenton or Philadelphia. He begged them not to attempt to go to the enemy. They declared it was not their intention, and that they would hang any man who would attempt it, and for that, if the enemy should come out in consequence of this revolt, they would turn back and fight them. "If that is your sentiments," said the General, "I'll not leave you, and if you won't allow me to march in your front, I'll follow in your rear."

This day, January 2, Colonels Steward and Richard Butler joined General Wayne in hopes they could turn them when they grew cooler, being much agitated with liquor when they went off; it being New Year's Day, they had drawn half a pint per man. The men have continued going off in small parties all day. About one o'clock, one hundred head of cattle came in from the eastward, which they drove off to their main body, which lay in a wood near Vealtown, leaving a few behind for use of the officers.

When we came to draw provisions and state stores this day, we found that near half the men of our regiment had remained.

The men went off very civilly last night to what might have been expected from such a mob. They did not attempt to plunder our officers' huts or insult them in the least, except those who were obstinate in opposing them. They did not attempt to take with them any part of the state stores, which appears to me a little extraordinary, for men when they get but little want more.

From "Extracts from the Letter-Books of Lieutenant Enos Reeves, of the Pennsylvania Line," *Pennsylvania Magazine of History and Biography*, Vol. XXI, 1891.

The trouble spread. A few weeks later at the Pompton Camp, three New Jersey regiments mutinied. Washington swiftly sent five hundred men under Major General Robert Howe to put it down. As Howe surrounded the camp, Dr. James Thacher observed the outcome:

FINDING THEMSELVES CLOSELY ENCIRCLED and unable to resist, they quietly submitted to the fate which awaited them. General Howe ordered that three of the ringleaders should be selected as victims for condign punishment. These unfortunate culprits were tried on the spot, Colonel Sprout being present of the court-martial, standing in the snow, and they were sentenced to be immediately shot. Twelve of the most guilty mutineers were next selected to be their executioners. This was a most painful task; being themselves guilty, they were greatly distressed with the duty imposed upon them and, when ordered to load, some of them shed tears.

The wretched victims, overwhelmed by the terrors of death, had neither time nor power to implore the mercy and forgiveness of their God, and such was their agonizing condition that no heart could refrain from emotions of sympathy and compassion. The first that suffered was a sergeant, and an old offender. He was led a few yards distance, and placed on his knees. Six of the executioners, at the signal given by an officer, fired, three aiming at the head and three at the breast, the other six reserving their fire in order to dispatch the victim should the first fire fail; it so happened, in this instance, the remaining six then fired, and life was instantly extinguished. The second criminal was, by the first fire, sent into eternity in an instant. The third, being less criminal by the recommendation of his officers, to his unspeakable joy, received a pardon. This tragical scene produced a dreadful shock and a salutary effect on the minds of the guilty soldiers. Never were men more completely humbled and penitent; tears of sorrow and of joy rushed from their eyes, and each one appeared to congratulate himself that his forfeit life had been spared.

The executions being finished, General Howe ordered

the former officers to take their stations and resume their commands.

From *A Military Journal*, Thacher, 1827.

30

The People Have Become Savage

When the Declaration of Independence was adopted, every colonist was forced to make a choice: to support the new revolutionary government, or to support Britain. Some fell between the two. They would try to stay neutral, and accept the outcome of the war whichever way it went.

The colonists who chose independence were called Patriots, or Whigs; those who chose Britain's side were called Loyalists, or Tories. Perhaps a third of the colonists may have been Loyalists, another third Patriots, and the last third neutral. Friends, neighbors, families were torn apart by their decisions. So powerful an upheaval as a revolution causes the rupture of old relationships and the deepest ties. The revolution was as much a civil war as a war with Britain.

The fact that there were so many Loyalists, strong enough to endanger the revolution, made the Patriots grimly determined to punish and destroy them. As early as 1774 the Loyalists were denounced as "infamous betrayers of their country." The Continental Congress encouraged local "committees of safety" to report their every move and terrify them into silence and inaction. Volunteer Patriots smashed their windows, hurled garbage, whipped, and tarred and feathered Loyalists. (Sometimes patriotism became a cover for repaying old grudges.) The states soon adopted laws to punish Toryism. The laws limited freedom of speech and movement, took away civil rights, isolated or banished Tories, confiscated their property, and even condemned to death people who stayed loyal to Britain and the king.

Every stage of the war produced ample evidence to confirm the Patriot view of Tories. They did prove to be a great danger. They spied and informed for the British, they furnished the redcoats with food and supplies, and thousands fought against Washington's forces. Loyalists were especially numerous on the southern front. As hatred deepened between the two sides, atrocities became common. Moses Hall, twenty-one, a North Carolina infantryman, helped defeat Tory troops supporting the British Colonel Tarleton on February 23, 1781. The young soldier describes the atrocity he witnessed, and its brutalizing effect upon himself:

THE EVENING AFTER our battle with the Tories, we having a considerable number of prisoners, I recollect a scene which made a lasting impression upon my mind. I was invited by some of my comrades to go and see

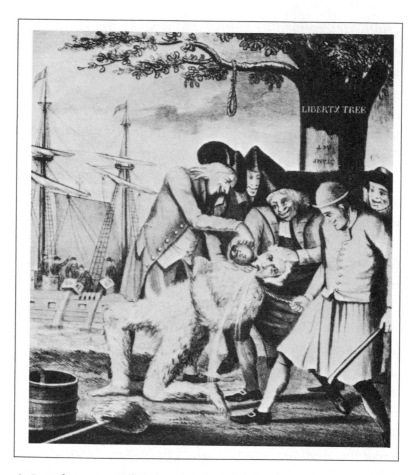

A British cartoon shows mean-looking Patriots forcing a tarred-and-feathered tax collector to drink the tea His Majesty King George III was taxing. Both Tories and Patriots were quick to violence in what became as much a civil war as a Revolution.

some of the prisoners. We went to where six were standing together. Some discussion taking place, I heard some of our men cry out, "Remember Buford" [site of a Tory atrocity], and the prisoners were immediately hewed to pieces with broadswords. At first I bore the scene without any emotion, but upon a moment's reflection, I felt such horror as I never did before nor have since, and, returning to my quarters and throwing myself upon my blanket, I contemplated the cruelties of war until overcome and unmanned by a distressing gloom from which I was not relieved until commencing our march next morning before day by moonlight. I came to Tarleton's camp, which he had just abandoned, leaving lively rail fires. Being on the left of the road as we marched along, I discovered lying upon the ground something with the appearance of a man. Upon approaching him, he proved to be a youth about sixteen who, having come out to view the British through curiosity, for fear he might give information to our troops, they had run him through with a bayonet and left him for dead. Though able to speak, he was mortally wounded. The sight of this unoffending boy, butchered rather than be encumbered in the [illegible] on the march, I assume, relieved me of my distressful feelings for the slaughter of the Tories, and I desired nothing so much as the opportunity of participating in their destruction.

From Revolutionary War Pension Applications, National Archives.

In South Carolina, James Collins observed three classes of Tories as he soldiered up and down the state during the hellishly hot summer of 1781:

THERE WAS A CLASS of Tories who, I believe, were Tories from principle. Another class believed it impossible for the cause of liberty to succeed and thought, in the end,

I Benedict Arnold Major General do acknowledge the UNITED STATES of AMERICA to be Free, Independent and Sovereign States, and declare that the people thereof owe no allegiance or obedience to George the Third, King of Great-Britain; and I renounce, refuse and abjure any allegiance or obedience to him; and I do Swear that I will, to the utmost of my power, support, maintain and defend the said United States against the said King George the Third, his heirs and successors, and his or their abettors, assistants and adherents, and will serve the said United States in the office of Major General which I now hold, with fidelity, according to the best of my skill and understanding. Sworn before me this 30th May 1778 at the Artillery Park Valley Forge B Arnold H Knox B Elliot

An oath of allegiance to the United States was demanded of all soldiers. This is General Benedict Arnold's oath, signed by him at Valley Forge in 1778. His turning traitor only a year later was a great shock to General Washington.

whatever they got they would be enabled to hold, and so become rich; they resorted to murdering and plundering and every means to get hold of property. Another class were Tories entirely through fear, and fit for nothing, only to be made tools of by the others, and all cowards, too.

There was another class of men amongst us, who pretended neutrality entirely on both sides; they pretended friendship to all and prayed, "Good God!"; "Good Devil!"; not knowing into whose hands they might fall. . . .

We would meet at a time and place appointed, probably at a church, schoolhouse, or some vacant building, generally in the afternoon, lay off our circuit and divide into two or more companies and set off after dark. Wherever we found any Tories, we would surround the house. One party would force the doors and enter, sword in hand, extinguish all the lights if there were any, and suffer no lights to be made, when we would commence hacking the man or men that were found in the house, threatening them with instant death, and occasionally making a furious stroke as if to dispatch them at once, but taking care to strike the wall or some object that was in the way, they generally being found crouched up in some corner, or about the beds.

Another party would mount the roof of the house and commence pulling it down. Thus, the dwelling house, smoke house, and kitchen, if any, were dismantled and torn down, at least to the joists. The poor fellows, perhaps expecting instant death, would beg hard for life, and make any promise on condition of being spared, while their wives or friends would join in their entreaties. . . . There were none of the poor fellows much hurt, only they were hacked about their heads and arms enough to bleed freely.

From *Autobiograpny*, Collins, 1859.

On the same front, the soldier William Pierce was horrified by the cruelty of the war between Patriot (Whig) and Tory:

SUCH SCENES of desolation, bloodshed and deliberate murder, I never was a witness to before! Wherever you turn the weeping widow and fatherless child pour out their melancholy tales to wound the feelings of humanity. The two opposite principles of Whiggism and To-ryism have set the people of this country to cutting each other's throats, and scarce a day passes but some poor deluded Tory is put to death at his door. For the want of civil government, the bands of society are totally dis-united, and the people, by copying the manners of the British, have become perfectly savage.

From *Magazine of American History*, Vol. VIII, 1881. William Pierce letter to St. George Tucker, July 20, 1781.

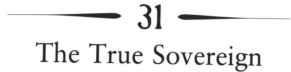

31

The True Sovereign

Late in the war the Marquis de Chastellux, while traveling in America, met Samuel Adams. In long conversation the two exchanged ideas on the nature of government. The expansion of the people's role in pol-itics—a major achievement of the Revolution—was new, and its benefits questionable to many. The French no-bleman told the radical democrat that he feared in time wealthy Americans would use their power to dominate the new republican government and throw the democ-racy off balance. Samuel Adams replied by explaining how the government of his own state, Massachusetts, was formed, giving the Frenchman insight into how the

*future national government might work. In his book
about his travels, the Marquis repeats what Adams told
him:*

I AM VERY SENSIBLE of the force of your objections; we
are not what we should be, we should labor rather for
the future than for the present moment. I build a country
house, and have infant children; I ought doubtless to
construct their apartments with an eye to the time in
which they shall be grown up and married, but we have
not neglected this precaution.

In the first place, I must inform you that this new
constitution was proposed and agreed to in the most
legitimate manner of which there is any example since
the days of Lycurgus. A committee chosen from the
members of the legislative body, then existing, and which
might be considered as a provisional government, was
named to prepare a new code of laws. As soon as it was
prepared, each county or district was required to name
a committee to examine this plan: it was recommended
to them to send it back, at the expiration of a certain
time, with their observations. These observations having
been discussed by the committee, and the necessary al-
terations made, the plan was sent back to each particular
committee. When they had all approved it, they received
orders to communicate it to the people at large, and to
demand their suffrages. If two-thirds of the voters approved it, it was to have the force of law, and be regarded
as the work of the people themselves; of two and twenty
thousand suffrages, a much greater proportion than two-
thirds was in favor of the new constitution.

165

Samuel Adams. A power in Boston politics, he shaped Revolutionary thought and action. He served in the Continental Congress and after the war was Governor of Massachusetts. In this 1771 oil painting by John Singleton Copley, Adams is pointing to the charter of Massachusetts.

Now these were the principles on which it was established: A state is never free but when each citizen is bound by no law whatever that he has not approved of, either by himself, or by his representatives; but to represent another man, it is necessary to have been elected by him; every citizen therefore should have a part in elections.

On the other hand, it would be in vain for the people to possess the right of electing representatives, were they restrained in the choice of them to a particular class; it is necessary therefore not to require too much property as a qualification for the representative of the people. Accordingly the house of representatives which form the legislative body, and the true sovereign, are the people themselves represented by their delegates.

Thus far the government is purely democratical; but it is the permanent and enlightened will of the people which should constitute law, and not the passions and sallies to which they are, too, subject. It is necessary to moderate their first emotions, and bring them to the test of enquiry and reflection. This is the important business entrusted with the governor and senate, who represent with us the negative power, vested in England in the upper house, and even in the Crown, with this difference only: that in our new constitution the senate has a right to reject a law, and the governor to suspend the promulgation, and return it for a reconsideration; but these forms complied with, if, after this fresh examination, the people persist in their resolution, and there is then not, as before, a mere majority, but two-thirds of the suffrages in favor of the law, the governor and senate are compelled to give it their sanction. Thus this power moderates without destroying the authority of the people, and such is the organization of our republic as to prevent the springs from breaking by too rapid a movement, without ever stopping them entirely.

Now it is here we have given all its weight to property.

A man must have a pretty considerable property to vote for a member of the senate; he must have a more considerable one to make himself eligible. Thus the democracy is pure and entirely in the assembly, which represents the sovereign; and the aristocracy, or, if you will, the optimacy, is to be found only in the moderating power, where it is the more necessary as men never watch more carefully over the state than when they have a great interest in its destiny.

As to the power of commanding armies, it ought neither to be vested in a great nor even in a small number of men: the governor alone can employ the forces by sea and land according to the necessity; but the land forces will consist only in the militia, which, as it is composed of the people themselves, can never act against the people.

From *Travels in North America*, 1780–82, Francois Jean,
Marquis de Chastellux, Vol. I, 1827.

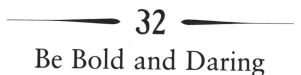

32

Be Bold and Daring

While the main battles of the revolution were fought on land, other American forces engaged the British at sea. In the early years of the war most of the naval action was carried on by privateers. A privateer was an ordinary merchant ship manned by a civilian crew. Guns were mounted on the deck. The goal was to capture British ships and take their cargo. The booty was then sold in port and the money divided among the ship's owners and officers by some agreement made in advance. This was a kind of large-scale private war, driven as much by profit as by patriotism. But it did great damage to British commerce and forced British squadrons to take on the privateers, who sank or captured about six hundred British ships, both commercial and military.

Of course the British navy was far superior to the small American one. (Only when the French navy came to America's aid did the balance shift.) The Continental navy at best commanded one hundred ships as against the nearly five hundred British. The Americans wisely never met the enemy in full battle. They stuck to convoy duty and raids upon single British frigates.

One of the most famous privateer captains was young Joshua Barney of Pennsylvania. He commanded the Hyder Ali, *commissioned by Philadelphia merchants to guard their shipping from British attack in Delaware Bay. In April 1782 Captain Barney fought the British brig* H.M.S. General Monk *commanded by Captain Rogers, and captured the larger vessel. It was renamed the* General Washington *and placed in the American navy. Barney's exploit was celebrated in a song written by the poet-editor Philip Freneau and published in the newspapers. Topical songs and ballads were very popular and circulated widely, often in broadsides:*

169

On Captain Barney's Victory
over the Ship *General Monk*

O'er the waste of waters cruising,
Long the *General Monk* had reigned;
All subduing, all reducing,
None her lawless rage restrained.
Many a brave and hearty fellow,
Yielding to this warlike foe,
When her guns began to bellow
Struck his humbled colors low.

But grown bold with long successes,
Leaving the wide watery way,
She a stranger to distresses,
Came to cruise within Cape May:
"Now we soon," said Captain Rogers,
"Shall their men of commerce meet;
In our hold we'll have them lodgers,
We shall capture half their fleet." . . .

Captain Barney then preparing,
Thus addressed his gallant crew:
"Now, brave lads, be bold and daring;
Let your hearts be firm and true;
This is a proud English cruiser,
Roving up and down the main;
We must fight her—must reduce her,
Though our decks be strewed with slain.

"Let who will be the survivor;
We must conquer or must die;
We must take her up the river,
Whate'er comes of you or I.

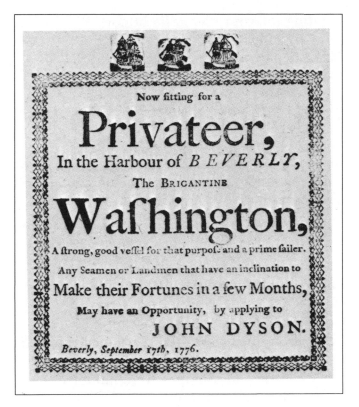

A poster used to recruit volunteers for service on a privateer. Many nations used privateers—cheaper than a navy—to harry the enemy in time of war.

Though she shows most formidable
With her eighteen pointed nines,
And her quarters clad in sable;
Let us balk her proud designs.

"With four nine pounders, and twelve sixes
We will face that daring band;
Let no dangers damp your courage,
Nothing can the brave withstand.

Fighting for your country's honor,
Now to gallant deeds aspire;
Helmsman, bear us down upon her;
Gunner, give the word to fire!"

Then yardarm and yardarm meeting,
Strait began the dismal fray;
Cannon mouths, each other greeting,
Belched their smoky flames away.
Soon the langrage, grape and chain shot,
That from Barney's cannons flew,
Swept the *Monk*, and cleared each round top,
Killed and wounded half her crew.

Captain Rogers strove to rally
But they from their quarters fled,
While the roaring *Hyder Ali*
Covered o'er his decks with dead.
When from their tops their dead men tumbled,
And the streams of blood did flow,
Then their proudest hopes were humbled
By their brave inferior foe.

All aghast, and all confounded,
They beheld their champions fall,
And their captain, sorely wounded,
Bade them quick for quarters call.
Then the *Monk*'s proud flag descended,
And her cannon ceased to roar;
By her crew no more defended,
She confessed the contest o'er.

Come, brave boys, and fill your glasses,
You have humbled one proud foe;
No brave action this surpasses,
Fame shall tell the nations so—

Thus be Britain's woes completed,
Thus abridged her cruel reign,
Till she ever, thus defeated,
Yields the sceptre of the main.

From *The Poems of Philip Freneau, Poet of the American Revolution,*
Frederick Lewis Pattee, ed., 1903.

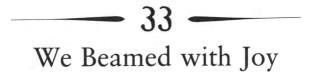

33

We Beamed with Joy

*It was effective support from the French that brought
the drawn-out war to its end. In July 1780 they sent
over General Rochambeau with some five thousand regulars, and in 1781, under Admiral de Grasse, a powerful
naval force arrived. France also lent more money to the
Americans for arms, equipment, food, and back pay
owed the troops.*

*Washington and the French conferred on strategy and
agreed to have their forces join in the Chesapeake Bay
region. Meanwhile the British general Lord Cornwallis
moved up to Virginia and camped on the York River at
Yorktown. The French fleet blocked the sea entrance to
Yorktown, which prevented Sir Henry Clinton's fleet
and army from sailing down from New York to rescue
Cornwallis. And the American and French troops blocked
the land entrance to the York peninsula, barring that*

escape route for Cornwallis. It was a classic maneuver that trapped the British.

On October 19, 1781, seeing his food and supplies melt away, and under steady bombardment from French and American guns, Cornwallis was forced to give up. He surrendered his entire army of seven thousand men. Dr. James Thacher was there to record his impressions of the surrender ceremony:

AT ABOUT TWELVE o'clock, the combined army was arranged and drawn up in two lines extending more than a mile in length. The Americans were drawn up in a line on the right side of the road, and the French occupied the left. At the head of the former, the great American commander, mounted on his noble courser, took his station, attended by his aides. At the head of the latter was posted the excellent Count Rochambeau and his suite. The French troops, in complete uniform, displayed a martial and noble appearance. Their band of music, of which the timbrel formed a part, is a delightful novelty, and produced, while marching to the ground, a most enchanting effect. The Americans, though not all in uniform, nor their dress so neat, yet exhibited an erect, soldierly air, and every countenance beamed with satisfaction and joy. The concourse of spectators from the country was prodigious, in point of numbers and probably equal to the military, but universal silence and order prevailed.

It was about two o'clock when the captive army advanced through the line formed for their reception. Every

A Currier & Ives print depicting announcement of the grand news: Cornwallis Is Taken at Yorktown! The dispatch is read from the steps of the State House (Independence Hall) in Philadelphia, October 23, 1781.

eye was prepared to gaze on Lord Cornwallis, the object of particular interest and solicitude, but he disappointed our anxious expectations. Pretending indisposition, he made General O'Hara his substitute as the leader of the army. The officer was followed by the conquered troops in a slow and solemn step, with shouldered arms, colors cased, and drums beating a British march. . . .

The royal troops, while marching through the line formed by the allied army, exhibited a decent and neat appearance, as respected arms and clothing. For their commander opened his store, and directed every soldier to be furnished with a new suit complete, prior to the

In Boston, a broadside appeals to the people to celebrate the victory at Yorktown with "A New Song," to be sung to "any one of the merriest tunes you can find."

capitulation. But in their line of march, we remarked a disorderly and unsoldierly conduct, their step was irregular, and their ranks frequently broken.

But it was in the field, when they came to the last act of the drama, that the spirit and pride of the British soldier was put to the severest test; here their mortification could not be concealed. Some of the platoon officers appeared to be exceedingly chagrined when giving the word, "Ground arms," and I am a witness that they performed this duty in a very unofficerlike manner, and that many of the soldiers manifested a sullen temper, throwing their arms on the pile with violence, as if determined to render them useless. This irregularity, however, was checked by the authority of General Lincoln. After having grounded their arms, and divested themselves of their accoutrements, the captive troops were conducted back to Yorktown and guarded by our troops till they could be removed to the place of their destination.

From *A Military Journal*, Thacher, 1827.

34

Never a Good War
or a Bad Peace

On the night of the surrender at Yorktown, an American colonel wrote, "I noticed that the officers and soldiers could scarcely talk for laughing, and they could scarcely walk for jumping and dancing and singing as they went." The men had fought for so many terrible years: This was their magnificent moment. An express rider galloped north to far-off Philadelphia to bring the glorious news to Congress. A frenzied celebration exploded. As the news spread through the states, illuminations, bonfires, rockets, roasted oxen, and overflowing liquor marked the festivities. It took more than a month for the news to reach London and the Downing Street residence of the British Prime Minister, Lord North. Asked how he took the news, a witness said, "As he would have taken a ball in the breast. For he opened his arms exclaiming wildly, as he paced up and down the apartment during a few minutes, 'Oh, God! It is all over!' "

There was sporadic fighting for a year more, but in reality the revolution had been won. Congress sent a peace commission abroad to negotiate a treaty. A final draft was signed on September 3, 1783. It signified Britain's acceptance of the colonies as an independent nation, the United States of America.

This was the first revolution of modern times against a monarchy and an empire. Many peoples the world over would aspire to the same aims and achievements. France, in 1789, was the first to follow, dethroning a king and establishing a republic. In the nineteenth century, almost every country in western Europe and Latin America would seek to reshape its political system after the model of the new American government. In the twentieth century it would happen again and again in Asia and in Africa.

From Paris, where he helped negotiate the treaty, Benjamin Franklin wrote home to his friend Joseph Banks, to comment on what the coming of peace might mean:

I JOIN WITH YOU most cordially in rejoicing at the return of peace. I hope it will be lasting, and that mankind will, at length, as they call themselves reasonable creatures, have reason and sense enough to settle their differences without cutting throats: For in my opinion, there never was a good war or a bad peace. What vast additions to the conveniences and comforts of living might mankind have acquired, if the money spent in wars had been employed in works of public utility! What an extension of agriculture, even to the tops of our mountains; what rivers rendered navigable or joined by canals; what bridges, aqueducts, new roads, and other public works, edifices, and improvements rendering England a complete paradise, might have been obtained by spending those millions in doing good, which in the last war have been spent in doing mischief; in bringing misery into thousands of families, and destroying the lives of so many thousands of working people, who might have performed the useful labor!

From Letter of July 27, 1783, *Benjamin Franklin, Complete Works,* John Bigelow, ed., 1887–89, Vol. X.

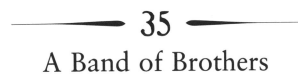

A Band of Brothers

So it was over. Eight years after the redcoats had fired upon the rebels at Lexington, it was time for the soldiers to go home: to clear overgrown fields and woods, to plant crops, to open the cobwebbed doors of shops, to clean the rusted tools of old trades. And once again to settle into family life, secure in the belief that the drums of war would not beat again.

They asked for their pay, but the penniless Congress could offer only promissory notes. Some of the officers, fearing Congress would forget any promise of money or land or pension after they disbanded, threatened armed revolt. Washington met with them, and begged them to do nothing that would "lessen the dignity or sully the glory" they had demonstrated to the world. His words touched their hearts and they voted their confidence in Congress.

There were many soldiers who did not wait for a

formal discharge. They simply walked off. Sergeant Jo-
seph Martin, dismissed in June 1783, recalls his last
hours in service:

"THE OLD MAN," our captain, came into our room . . .
and handed us our discharges, or rather furloughs. . . . I
confess, after all, that my anticipation of the happiness
I should experience upon such a day as this was not re-
alized. . . . We had lived together as a family of brothers
for several years (setting aside some little family squab-
bles, like most other families); had shared with each
other the hardships, dangers, and sufferings incident to
a soldier's life, had sympathized with each other in trouble and sickness; had assisted in bearing each other's
burdens, or strove to make them lighter by council and
advice; had endeavored to conceal each other's faults,
or make them appear in as good a light as they would
bear. In short, the soldiery, each in his particular circle
of acquaintance, were as strict a band of brotherhood
as Masons, and I believe as faithful to each other. And
now we were to be (the greater part of us) parted
forever, as unconditionally separated as though the grave
lay between us. This, I say, was the case with the most;
I will not say all. There were as many genuine misan-
thropists among the soldiers . . . as of any other class of
people whatever. . . . But we were young men and had
warm hearts. I question if there was a corps in the army
that parted with more regret than ours did, the New
Englanders in particular. Ah! it was a serious time!

Some of the soldiers went off for home the same day

181

that their fetters were knocked off; others stayed and got their final settlement certificates, which they sold to procure decent clothing and money sufficient to enable them to pass with decency through the country, and to appear something like themselves when they arrived among their friends. I was among those. . . . I . . . sold some of them and purchased some decent clothing and then set off.

From *A Narrative of Some of the Adventures, Dangers and Sufferings of a Revolutionary Soldier*, Joseph P. Martin, 1830.

As for General Washington, his farewell to the officers of his vanishing army came in a final meeting in New York at the Fraunces Tavern on Pearl Street, on December the fourth. Colonel Benjamin Tallmadge was there, and left this description of that moving hour:

WE HAD BEEN ASSEMBLED but a few moments when His Excellency entered the room. His emotion, too strong to be concealed, seemed to be reciprocated by every officer present.

After partaking of a slight refreshment, in almost breathless silence, the general filled his glass with wine, and turning to his officers, he said, "With a heart full of love and gratitude, I now take leave of you. I most devoutly wish that your latter days may be as prosperous and happy as your former ones have been glorious and honorable."

After the officers had taken a glass of wine, General

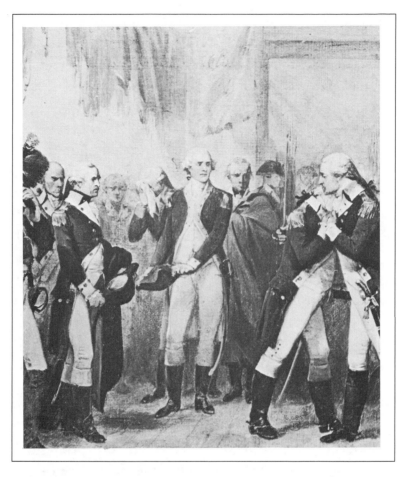

Saying good-bye to his few officers still in service, Washington (at far right) tearfully embraces each one separately. This last parting took place at Fraunces Tavern in New York in December 1783.

Washington said, "I cannot come to each of you, but shall feel obliged if each of you will come and take me by the hand."

General Knox, being nearest to him, turned to the

commander in chief, who, suffused in tears, was incapable of utterance, but grasped his hand, when they embraced each other in silence. In the same affectionate manner, every officer in the room marched up to, kissed, and parted with his general in chief.

Such a scene of sorrow and weeping I had never before witnessed, and hope I may never be called upon to witness again. . . . Not a word was uttered to break the solemn silence . . . or to interrupt the tenderness of the . . . scene. The simple thought that we were then about to part from the man who had conducted us through a long and bloody war, and under whose conduct the glory and independence of our country had been achieved, and that we should see his face no more in this world, seemed to me utterly insupportable.

But the time of separation had come, and waving his hand to his grieving children around him, he left the room, and passing through a corps of light infantry who were paraded to receive him, he walked silently on to Whitehall, where a barge was in waiting. We all followed in mournful silence to the wharf, where a prodigious crowd had assembled to witness the departure of the man who, under God, had been the great agent in establishing the glory and independence of these United States. As soon as he was seated, the barge put off into the river, and when out in the stream, our great and beloved General waved his hat and bid us a silent adieu.

From Memoir, Benjamin Tallmadge, 1904.

36

This Country
Has So Many Charms

The Americans had fought for the idea of freedom, not just for a piece of land. And America itself became an idea, a dream, in the minds of people everywhere. To many the new-made democracy was one of the greatest steps in the course of human development. A voice from America shouted "Liberty!" and the echo of it sounded in the ear of the oppressed and gave them hope.

Michel-Guillaume Jean de Crèvecœur, a French traveler and agriculturist who wrote under the pen name J. Hector St. John, had emigrated to America in 1754, settling on a farm in New York State. He published a book in 1782 called Letters from an American Farmer. *In it he told his readers of the opportunities for a new life in America, singing the praises of "this smiling country." Note the contrast between the optimistic tone of this immigrant and the gloomy experiences recorded by Gottfried Mittelberger ("They Cry Out for Home," pages 5–14), who came to America at about the same time. Crèvecœur, too, went back to Europe, in 1780, while the revolution was not yet won, and returned to New York in 1783 as French consul. This passage from his popular book, now a classic, reveals why the immigrants to come expected their new land to be almost an Eden:*

EUROPE CONTAINS hardly any other distinctions but lords and tenants; this fair country alone is settled by freeholders, the possessors of the soil they cultivate, members of the government they obey, and the framers of their own laws, by means of their representatives. . . .

There is no wonder that this country has so many charms, and presents to Europeans so many temptations to remain in it. A traveler in Europe becomes a stranger as soon as he quits his own kingdom; but it is otherwise here. We know, properly speaking, no strangers. This is every person's country. The variety of our soils, situations, climates, governments, and produce hath something which must please everybody. No sooner does an European arrive, no matter of what condition, than his eyes are opened upon the fair prospect. He hears his language spoke. He retraces many of his own country manners. He perpetually hears the names of families and towns with which he is acquainted. He sees happiness and prosperity in all places disseminated. He meets with hospitality, kindness, and plenty everywhere. He beholds hardly any poor. He seldom hears of punishments and executions, and he wonders at the elegance of our towns, those miracles of industry and freedom. He cannot admire enough our rural districts, our convenient roads, good taverns, and our many accommodations. He involuntarily loves a country where everything is so lovely. . . . He does not find, as in Europe, a crowded society where every place is overstocked. He does not feel that perpetual collision of parties, that difficulty of beginning, that contention which oversets so many.

There is room for everybody in America. Has he any particular talent or industry? He exerts it in order to procure a livelihood, and it succeeds. Is he a merchant? The avenues of trade are infinite. Is he eminent in any respect? He will be employed and respected. Does he love a country life? Pleasant farms present themselves. He may purchase what he wants, and thereby become an American farmer. Is he a laborer, sober and industrious? He need not go many miles, nor receive many informations before he will be hired, well fed at the table of his employer, and paid four or five times more than he can get in Europe. Does he want uncultivated lands? Thousands of acres present themselves, which he may purchase cheap. Whatever be his talents or inclinations, if they are moderate, he may satisfy them. . . .

An European, when he first arrives, seems limited in his intentions, as well as in his views; but he very suddenly alters his scale. Two hundred miles formerly appeared a very great distance. It is now but a trifle. He no sooner breathes our air than he forms schemes and embarks in designs he never would have thought of in his own country. There the plenitude of society confines many useful ideas, and often extinguishes the most laudable schemes which here ripen into maturity. Thus Europeans become Americans. . . .

Let me select one as an epitome of the rest. He is hired, he goes to work, and works moderately. Instead of being employed by a haughty person, he finds himself with his equal, placed at the substantial table of the farmer, or else at an inferior one as good. His wages are

Jean de Crèvecœur, French traveler, agriculturist, and memoirist. His insight into the American character and his vision of its development proved to be quite accurate.

high, his bed is not like that bed of sorrow on which he used to lie. If he behaves with propriety and is faithful, he is caressed and becomes, as it were, a member of the family. He begins to feel the effects of a sort of resurrection. Hitherto he had not lived, but simply vegetated. He now feels himself a man, because he is treated as such. The laws of his own country had overlooked him in his insignificancy. The laws of this cover him with their mantle. Judge what an alteration there must arise in the mind and thoughts of this man. He begins to forget his former servitude and dependence. His heart involuntarily swells and glows. This first swell inspires him with those new thoughts which constitute an American. . . .

What an epoch in this man's life! He is become a freeholder, from, perhaps, a German boor—he is now an American, a Pennsylvanian, an English subject. He is naturalized. His name is enrolled with those of the other citizens of the province. Instead of being a vagrant, he has a place of residence. He is called the inhabitant of such a county, or of such a district, and for the first time in his life counts for something, for hitherto he had been a cipher. I only repeat what I have heard many say, and no wonder their hearts should glow, and be agitated with a multitude of feelings, not easy to describe. From nothing to start into being, from a servant to the rank of a master, from being the slave of some despotic prince, to become a free man, invested with lands, to which every municipal blessing is annexed! What a change indeed! It is in consequence of that change that he becomes an American.

This great metamorphosis has a double effect; it extinguishes all his European prejudices. He forgets that mechanism of subordination, that servility of disposition which poverty had taught him; and sometimes he is apt to forget it too much, often passing from one extreme to the other. If he is a good man, he forms schemes of future prosperity. He proposes to educate his children better than he has been educated himself. He thinks of future modes of conduct, feels an ardor to labor he never felt before. Pride steps in, and leads him to everything that the laws do not forbid. He respects them. With a heartfelt gratitude he looks toward the east, toward that insular government from whose wisdom all his new felicity is derived, and under whose wings and protection he now lives. These reflections constitute him the good man and the good subject.

Ye poor Europeans, ye, who sweat and work for the great—ye, who are obliged to give so many sheaves to the church, so many to your lords, so many to your government, and have hardly any left for yourselves—ye, who are held in less estimation than favorite hunters or useless lapdogs—ye, who only breathe the air of nature because it cannot be withheld from you; it is here that ye can conceive the possibility of those feelings I have been describing; it is here the laws of naturalization

On September 17, 1787, the draft Constitution won final approval of the convention delegates. Two days later, on Wednesday, September 19, this Philadelphia newspaper printed the text, beginning with the Preamble in large type.

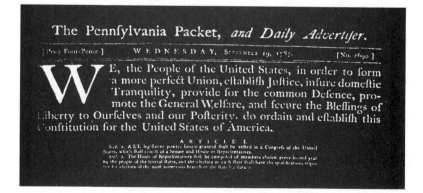

invite every one to partake of our great labors and felicity, to till unrented, untaxed lands!

From *Letters from an American Farmer*, Jean de Crèvecœur, 1782.

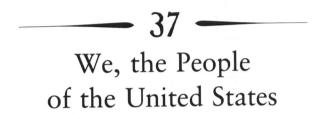

37

We, the People
of the United States

*How would the new nation be governed? During the
Revolutionary War the thirteen sovereign states had come
together for joint defense and to conduct a common
foreign policy. But each insisted on the right to rule itself
and refused to surrender its sovereignty to the Confederation. That government had been set up by the Articles
of Confederation, adopted in 1781. It rapidly proved
too weak and inadequate. The states quarreled among
themselves over boundary lines, over tariffs, over court
decisions; and hard times deepened the bitterness. A
strong central authority was badly needed to coordinate
interest and ensure order.*

    *Something had to be done, and quickly. The states
agreed that a national convention should meet in Philadelphia to strengthen the federal government so it could*

better meet the needs of the union. In May, 1787, fifty-five delegates from all the states met, with George Washington presiding. Over half the men were under forty; Benjamin Franklin, at age eighty-two, was by far the oldest.

The delegates threw aside the old articles and wrote a completely new Constitution during sixteen weeks of a hot summer. Out of their deliberations came a document whose wisdom, practical ingenuity, and vitality armed the new nation for a turbulent future.

Here is the preamble, which consists of two brief parts. The first defines the source of authority from which the Constitution is derived. The second defines the objects for which the Constitution and the government based upon it are created. The concept of "the people" as the source of power would undergo broader definition as time passed, giving new life to the Constitution in every generation:

WE, THE PEOPLE of the United States, in order to form a more perfect union, establish justice, insure domestic tranquility, provide for the common defence, promote the general welfare, and secure the blessings of liberty to ourselves and our posterity, do ordain and establish this Constitution for the United States of America.

The diversity of opinions and prejudices, the clash of regional and economic interests, the varying philosophical views, made agreement on this basic document almost impossible. Luckily, Benjamin Franklin shared with

Washington the task of conciliating the delegates, holding them together to complete the great work. As Franklin was too infirm to take the floor, his few speeches were read by James Wilson. But on the floor and off, he stressed the need for compassion and humility with that homely charm and wit that had made him so great an asset in diplomacy.

When the delegates reached a final draft, Franklin spoke to them, urging all to sign it. On September 17, 1787, the day of the signing of the Constitution, the old man rose and asked the convention to listen while Wilson read these words that would be reprinted in more than fifty newspapers. They would exert the most decisive influence during the intense ratification debate in the states:

I CONFESS that I do not entirely approve of this Constitution at present, but, Sir, I am not sure I shall never approve it: For having lived long, I have experienced many instances of being obliged, by better information or fuller consideration, to change opinions even on important subjects, which I once thought right, but found to be otherwise. It is therefore that the older I grow the more apt I am to doubt my own judgment, and to pay more respect to the judgment of others. Most men, indeed, as well as most sects in religion, think themselves in possession of all truth, and that wherever others differ from them it is so far error. . . . But though many private persons think almost as highly of their own infallibility as of that of their sect, few express it so naturally as a certain French lady who, in a little dispute with her sister, said, I don't know how it happens, sister, but I meet with nobody but myself that's always in the right.

In these sentiments, Sir, I agree to this Constitution, with all its faults, if they are such; because I think a general government necessary for us, and there is no form of government but what may be a blessing to the people if well administered; and I believe further that this is likely to be well administered for a course of years, and can only end in despotism, as other forms have done before it, when the people shall become so corrupted as to need despotic government, being incapable of any other.

I doubt, too, whether any other convention we can obtain may be able to make a better Constitution: for when you assemble a number of men to have the advantage of their joint wisdom, you inevitably assemble with those men all their prejudices, their passions, their errors of opinion, their local interests, and their selfish views. From such an assembly can a perfect production be expected? It therefore astonishes me, Sir, to find this system approaching so near to perfection as it does; and I think it will astonish our enemies, who are waiting with confidence to hear that our councils are confounded, like those of the builders of Babel, and that our states are on the point of separation, only to meet hereafter for the purpose of cutting one another's throats.

Thus I consent, Sir, to this Constitution because I expect no better, and because I am not sure that it is not the best. The opinions I have had of its errors I

Washington presiding over the Constitutional Convention in the earliest known engraving of the meeting.

sacrifice to the public good. I have never whispered a syllable of them abroad. Within these walls they were born, and here they shall die. If every one of us in returning to our constituents were to report the objections he has had to it, and use his influence to gain partisans in support of them, we might prevent its being generally received, and thereby lose all the salutary effects and great advantages resulting naturally in our favor among foreign nations, as well as among ourselves, from our real or apparent unanimity.

Much of the strength and efficiency of any government, in procuring and securing happiness to the people depends on opinion, on the general opinion of the goodness of that government as well as of the wisdom and integrity of its governors. I hope, therefore, that for our own sakes, as a part of the people, and for the sake of our posterity, we shall act heartily and unanimously in recommending this Constitution, wherever our influence may extend, and turn our future thoughts and endeavors to the means of having it well administered.

On the whole, Sir, I cannot help expressing a wish that every member of the convention, who may still have objections to it, would with me on this occasion doubt a little of his own infallibility, and to make manifest our unanimity, put his name to this instrument.

The American Museum, Philadelphia, December, 1787.

——— • 38 • ———

A Bill of Rights

When the newly drafted Constitution circulated in the states for ratification, the strongest criticism during the debates was its lack of a specific Bill of Rights. Having a Bill of Rights was an ancient English tradition, going back to the Magna Carta of 1215. Later, again and again, the British had obtained from their rulers dec-

larations of rights to protect their civil liberties. American colonials had often cited them when protesting arbitrary acts of British officials. That is why most states put a Bill of Rights into their own constitutions.

At the Constitutional Convention, many assumed that the individual was already protected by the states' bills. And in the draft of the Constitution there were scattered provisions of some important liberties. Still, many thought the Constitution did not go far enough. Jefferson said that a Bill of Rights "is what the people are entitled to against every government on earth . . . and what no just government should refuse." He and others argued that civil liberties should be made into constitutional rights.

So when the first Congress convened in 1787, debate started on constitutional amendments sponsored by James Madison of Virginia. After committee work on a Bill of Rights in both House and Senate, a final draft, adopted on September 25, proposed twelve constitutional amendments. Ten of these were ratified by the requisite three fourths of the states, and the Bill of Rights became part of the fundamental law of the land on December 15, 1791. They guarantee freedoms for individuals that no government can take away. The First Amendment, for instance, provides for freedom of religion, speech, and press, the right to peaceful assembly, and the right to petition government to obtain redress of grievances.

AMENDMENT I.

Congress shall make no law respecting an establishment of religion, or prohibiting the free exercise thereof; or abridging the freedom of speech, or of the press; or the right of the people peaceably to assemble, and to petition the government for a redress of grievances.

AMENDMENT II.

A well regulated militia being necessary to the security of a free state, the right of the people to keep and bear arms, shall not be infringed.

AMENDMENT III.

No soldier shall in time of peace be quartered in any house, without the consent of the owner, nor in time of war, but in a manner to be prescribed by law.

AMENDMENT IV.

The right of the people to be secure in their persons, houses, papers, and effects, against unreasonable searches and seizures, shall not be violated, and no warrants shall issue, but upon probable cause, supported by oath or affirmation, and particularly describing the place to be searched, and the persons or things to be seized.

AMENDMENT V.

No person shall be held to answer for a capital, or otherwise infamous crime, unless on a presentment or indictment of a grand jury, except in cases arising in the land or naval forces, or in the militia, when in actual service in time of war or public danger; nor shall any person be subject for the same offence to be twice put in jeopardy of life or limb; nor shall be compelled in any criminal case to be a witness against himself, nor be deprived of life, liberty, or property, without due process of law; nor shall private property be taken for public use, without just compensation.

AMENDMENT VI.

In all criminal prosecutions, the accused shall enjoy the right to a speedy and public trial, by an impartial jury of the state and district wherein the crime shall have been committed, which district shall have been previously ascertained by law, and to be informed of the nature and cause of the accusation; to be confronted with the witnesses against him; to have compulsory process for obtaining witnesses in his favor, and to have the assistance of counsel for his defence.

AMENDMENT VII.

In suits at common law, where the value in controversy shall exceed twenty dollars, the right of trial by jury shall be preserved, and no fact tried by a jury, shall be otherwise re-examined in any court of the United States, than according to the rules of the common law.

AMENDMENT VIII.

Excessive bail shall not be required, nor excessive fines imposed, nor cruel and unusual punishments inflicted.

AMENDMENT IX.

The enumeration in the Constitution, of certain rights, shall not be construed to deny or disparage others retained by the people.

Amendment X.

The powers not delegated to the United States by the Constitution, nor prohibited by it to the states, are reserved to the states respectively, or to the people.

The Bill of Rights can be only a paper barrier against the exercise of unjust power. History demonstrates how much depends upon the willingness of the legislative, executive, and judicial branches of government to respect those rights. And above all, on the vigilance of the people themselves to protect their liberties. Without them an open, free society cannot endure.

A NOTE ON SOURCES

Early on, many participants in the American Revolution, aware of the worldwide significance of the struggle, made and kept records of the events they were a part of. Only a few years after victory, the first slim collection of documents of the revolution appeared. As the mountain of source material piled higher and higher, multivolume editions were published. Scholars pored over contemporary newspapers, handbills, pamphlets, memoirs, letters, legislative reports, diaries, journals, and record books, and fanned out to explore the manuscripts deposited in historical societies, as well as in trunks and attics. Even today—two hundred years after the revolution—material comes to light in some dusty family closet or remote local archive to illuminate a corner of the story.

For those who wish to dig deeper into documents, here are some suggestions. John C. Dann's *The Revolution Remembered*, University of Chicago Press, 1980, contains eyewitness accounts drawn from applications of war veterans for pensions made possible by an 1832 act of Congress. In most cases the ex-soldiers told their stories to a court clerk or reporter, a method that provides us with something like the oral histories that have become so popular in recent times.

Dennis P. Ryan's *A Salute to Courage*, Columbia University Press, 1979, includes excerpts from diaries, letters, and journals written by officers of the Continental army and navy. Hugh F. Rankin, in his *The American Revolution*, Putnam, 1964, gives us a narrative account of those years, studded by a great many passages from the firsthand impressions left by soldiers, civilians, generals, and statesmen. At greater length, George F. Scheer and the same Hugh Rankin take a similar approach in *Rebels and Redcoats*, World, 1957. One of the more massive collections of documents was edited by two distinguished historians, Henry Steele Commager and Richard B. Morris; called *The Spirit of 'Seventy-Six*, Harper, 1967, it runs to over thirteen hundred large and closely printed pages.

Some readers interested in certain aspects of revolutionary times, such as the role of Blacks or Native Americans, or Jews or women or working people, can turn for additional documents to more specialized collections focusing on the histories of those groups. The reader caught by the personality of a Tom Paine, a Jefferson, a Washington, an Adams (any one of them), or scores of other notables can find their personal and official documents in collections devoted solely to the individual. To satisfy a more general interest in the revolutionary era and its many facets, there are many bibliographies any librarian will be glad to show you.

A delightful and useful path to the revolutionary era can be followed in those volumes that show the horizontal linkage of people and events. That is, you can find out who was doing what in any particular year not only in war and politics, but in the arts and sciences, in religion, technology, sports, fashion, popular entertainment. Try *The Encyclopedia of American Facts and Dates*, Gorton Carruth, ed., Crowell, 1956, or *The Timetable of American History*, Laurence Urdang, ed., Simon & Schuster, 1981. If you want to extend your scan to the world's horizons there is *The Timetables of History*, Bernard Grun, ed., Simon & Schuster, 1982.

Index

(Page references to illustrations and their captions are in *italics*.)

209